IN PLAIN VIEW

"With respect and insight, Judy Stavisky takes readers into the everyday experiences of Amish women, from shopping at Costco and managing a schoolroom to choosing fabrics and preparing to host Sunday church. Stavisky has a remarkable eye for detail and a keen sense of what, amid all the activity, is truly significant. Some aspects of Amish life may be in plain view, but you'll see them more clearly after reading this book."

—STEVEN M. NOLT, interim director and senior scholar at the Young Center for Anabaptist and Pietist Studies at Elizabethtown College and coauthor of *Amish Grace: How Forgiveness Transcended Tragedy*

"Judy Stavisky brings readers into the lives of Lancaster County Amish women, revealing the heart of Amish life. 'Simplicity brings satisfaction,' one Lancaster Amish woman tells her, but as *In Plain View* makes clear, there's little that is simple about the practical simplicity of Amish life."

—KAREN M. JOHNSON-WEINER, distinguished service professor emerita in the Anthropology Department at SUNY Potsdam and author of *All about the Amish* and *The Lives of Amish Women*

"Slip into the simple life in *In Plain View*, as Judy Stavisky shares her observations, wise and winsome, gleaned from driving Amish women on their everyday errands. Just ordinary women, yet to those of us on the outside, they live quite extraordinary lives. A lovely book."

—SUZANNE WOODS FISHER, bestselling author of *Amish Peace: Simple Wisdom for a Complicated World*

"Judy Stavisky does a remarkable job describing what it's like for women who were born and raised and are living their lives within the Amish culture. The real-life stories and conversations that took place between Stavisky and her Amish friends will make you laugh, cry, and rejoice. Most importantly, the author will leave you with a deeper desire to live a more healthy and simple life."

—**JOE KEIM**, author of *My People, the Amish*

"*In Plain View* grabbed hold of my attention and wouldn't let go. A wonderful book! Anyone interested in the Amish is sure to enjoy reading it."

—**KATE LLOYD**, bestselling author of *A Lancaster Family Christmas*

"In *In Plain View*, Judy Stavisky takes you behind the scenes of Amish life, revealing in intricate detail the whos, hows, whats, and whys of the Amish way. Through her special vantage point as a driver, acquaintance, and friend to Amish women, she provides an enlightening and entertaining look into life in the world's largest Amish community. Definitely worth reading, even if you feel you know the Amish well."

—**ERIK WESNER**, founder of the Amish America website and YouTube channel

IN PLAIN VIEW

—— *The Daily Lives of Amish Women* ——

JUDY STAVISKY

HERALD
PRESS

Harrisonburg, Virginia

Herald Press
PO Box 866, Harrisonburg, Virginia 22803
www.HeraldPress.com

Library of Congress Cataloging-in-Publication Data
Names: Stavisky, Judy, author.
Title: In plain view : the daily lives of Amish women / Judy Stavisky.
Description: Harrisonburg : Herald Press, 2022. | Includes bibliographical references.
Identifiers: LCCN 2022009608 | ISBN 9781513809816 (hardcover)
Subjects: LCSH: Amish women—Religious life. | Amish women—Social life and
    customs. | BISAC: RELIGION / Christianity / Amish | SOCIAL SCIENCE /
    Women's Studies
Classification: LCC BX8129.A5 S73 2022 | DDC 289.7082—dc23/eng/20220316
LC record available at https://lccn.loc.gov/2022009608

Study guides are available for many Herald Press titles at www.HeraldPress.com.

IN PLAIN VIEW
© 2022 by Judy Stavisky, Harrisonburg, Virginia 22803. 800-245-7894.
    All rights reserved.
Library of Congress Control Number: 2022009608
International Standard Book Number: 978-1-5138-0981-6 (hardcover)

Printed in United States of America
All photos used with permission. Photographs by Dennis L. Hughes are from
    Photographs of the Amish, Hess Archives, Elizabethtown College.
Cover photo by Dennis L. Hughes
Cover and interior design by Merrill Miller

26 25 24 23 22   10 9 8 7 6 5 4 3 2 1

TABLE OF CONTENTS

Foreword

ABOUT TEN YEARS ago, I received a call from a Judy Stavisky, who asked if she could attend one of my courses on Amish life at Elizabethtown College. I was skeptical. After similar requests in the past, visitors typically dropped out once they realized this course was not for those with a casual tourist's interest but one that would delve into the deeper layers of Amish culture. Yet Stavisky seemed unusually serious and persuasive. I explained that the only Amish course I was teaching that semester was a three-hour evening seminar. No problem—she would be there. When I learned that she lived in Philadelphia and would travel to Elizabethtown by train—arriving late afternoon and returning home about midnight—I was delighted to have her on board. Clearly she was invested and eager to learn about Amish culture.

Our friendship, which grew over the next few years, paved the way for this book. As she explains in the introduction, I eventually asked her to gather information on the purchasing practices of Amish women for a book that I was revising. Unfortunately, I never completed the project. But happily, that data, along with the bountiful information that she gathered from visits with Amish friends, morphed into the book you now hold in your hands.

Stavisky's research began with old-fashioned bartering. She provided free rides for Amish women in exchange for talk time. Amish women are adept at driving a horse and buggy for local travel, but for longer trips, they often hire the services of a car owned and driven by a non-Amish neighbor. Her free rides for their free talk struck a mutual bargain. And the rides soon ballooned into home and school visits and invitations to participate in the daily lives of the Amish women in this community.

In Plain View is grounded on trust. Amish women are quick to smell the scent of counterfeit. If her Amish friends had detected that, they would have dropped their friendship. Stavisky didn't break or compromise that trust; she carefully describes the people who appear in the text without revealing their identity.

It is those friendships that nurtured this wonderful book. In the hours spent together in her car, Stavisky developed deep and rich ties with her Amish passengers. These ties grew into genuine, mutual friendships that fostered the intimacy and authenticity that sets this book apart from the multitudes of Amish-themed books that have soaked up printers' ink in recent decades—the so-called bonnet novels, tourist booklets, and academic tomes that focus on topics like *Rumspringa* or business, as well as others that explore Amish life in a particular state or region of the country.

When some academics write about Amish society, they use the jargon of their discipline, with its theories, methods, and hypotheses, creating a distance between readers and the Amish people they hope to better understand. But Stavisky, like an Amish woman baking a pie, starts from scratch. She brings a freshness, an open mind, and an insatiable curiosity that invites readers in to this world hidden to so many. Her engaging, warmhearted style signals profound respect for the women she met.

This book is distinctive for its meticulous focus on the details of everyday living. Learning, for example, that an Amish woman with a household of nine makes at least 180 plates of food a week—not to mention washing all the dirty dishes—tells us a lot about one small part of their daily routine. Such details provide us with an intimate portrait of authentic Amish life.

In many ways, *In Plain View* is a kaleidoscope of fascinating mini stories. The crisp, clear, easy-to-understand narrative is a delight to read. And that's because Amish women do most of the talking on virtually every page. This book is a pleasure to read for all these reasons—so pleasurable that it's hard to put it down.

—Donald Kraybill, bestselling author of *The Riddle of Amish Culture* and Senior Fellow Emeritus at Elizabethtown College's Young Center for Anabaptist and Pietist Studies

The Backstory

"WE KNOW MUCH more about you than you do about us," an Amish mother of six assured me.

At first glance, the silhouettes of Amish women in Lancaster County seem identical. Dresses in indistinguishable muted colors, stitched from look-alike sewing patterns. Black half-aprons ("belt aprons") wrapped around their waists and fastened at the back with five horizontal straight pins. An ethereal heart-shaped covering resting lightly on each woman's head.

One might assume that Amish women who conform to their community's narrow dress standards have little difference between them. But as I have learned, that assumption could not be further from the truth. Dressing the same does not equate to *being* the same.

Over the years, I have met effusive and witty Amish mothers and others who are tentative and reserved. I have accompanied Amish women who confidently maneuver a shopping cart through a cavernous Costco store. And I have shopped with women who were visibly uneasy whenever they left their insular community.

I have been curious about the Amish since my first purchase at a Lancaster County, Pennsylvania, farm stand decades ago. Within an hour's drive from downtown Philadelphia, rustic roadside booths teeming with homegrown produce and tempting baked goods dot the countryside. In contrast to the city's hustle, Amish life seems wholesome, enviable, even idyllic.

But sampling Amish life does not require leaving the city. Reading Terminal Market, the historic food emporium in the heart of Philadelphia, hosts several Amish vendors from rural communities in Chester and Lancaster Counties. Many Philly visitors have their first interactions with the Amish when purchasing their buttery soft pretzels or gooey fruit pies at the city's largest indoor public market. During my visits to Reading Terminal over forty years, I have observed the Amish patiently waiting on inquisitive tourists. I often wondered what the Amish thought about those curious sightseers.

When asked about the thousands of yearly visitors to Reading Terminal, an eighteen-year-old deli counter assistant, the daughter of an Amish friend, looked amused.

She shared, "Some out-of-town customers assume I am dressed in a costume," as if she were a reenactor in a living history museum.

Over the years, my curiosity about the Amish evolved and sharpened. When Saturday weather permitted, my husband and I would secure our ten-speed bicycles to the family's Subaru and drive to the closest Amish settlement, outside of Morgantown, Pennsylvania. We would then meander on our bicycles for hours. Observing Amish life from the seat of a two-wheeler seemed less invasive than gawking through a

car window. A cyclist can inconspicuously catch glimpses of daily routines from the perch of a bicycle seat—Amish mothers and daughters meticulously clipping laundry to lengthy clotheslines, fathers and sons maneuvering mule and horse teams through dusty fields, women and children carefully tending bountiful vegetable plots and flower gardens.

Peddling through pristine Amish hamlets, I noted the absence of power lines connecting homes to the electrical grid. I waved discreetly to Amish children peeking at me through the open back flap of their family's gray-topped buggy, delighted when they gestured back. My husband and I sought out the hand-lettered signs that indicate fresh brown eggs or newly dug potatoes for sale "back at the house." Each farm stand and backdoor offered a peek into Amish life that intrigued me and drew me closer.

Several years ago, I reached out to a professor at Elizabethtown College in Pennsylvania, an internationally known Amish scholar. Elizabethtown lies in the northwest corner of Lancaster County, well-known for its proximity to "Amish country," and is located about two hours from my home. The professor taught in-depth courses on the Amish, and I enthusiastically became one of his adult students. After sharing my interest in learning about the Amish from a more personal perspective, he suggested I assist him in collecting information on the purchasing practices of Amish women for a book he was updating.

Drawing on his close ties within the Amish community, the professor sent letters introducing me to several families. His messages provided personal information about me that he knew would interest Amish women: where I lived (Philadelphia), how long I had been married (thirty-five years), and how many children we raised (one). I learned much later, after meeting several Amish mothers, that they felt heavyhearted for me as a parent of only one child.

"In our culture, we would feel sorry for a child who grows up without brothers and sisters," admitted one Amish mother of seven.

The Elizabethtown College professor's introductory letter to his long-time Amish friends proposed the following: I would provide free transportation to Amish women for their shopping trips if they, in turn, would permit me to gently inquire about their purchases and their lives. Every woman who received a letter agreed to the arrangement.

Over time, several sisters, mothers, grandmothers, aunts, daughters, sons, and one husband joined me, dutifully securing themselves into seatbelts in my compact SUV. During each shopping trip, the car's empty trunk and any vacant seats would quickly reach capacity. Seeking additional stowage, we wedged jumbo packs of paper towels and industrial sized laundry detergent between the passengers' feet while balancing twenty-five-pound sacks of unbleached flour and gallon tubs of unsulfured baking molasses on assorted passengers' laps.

> **Amish children often** experience car sickness as passengers in automobiles. They find the continuous motion and lack of fresh air disagreeable.

"We can always fit more people and purchases in a buggy than a car. We can squish, sit on each other's laps, and stack our purchases high. And sitting close makes it warmer in the cold weather, too," one of my Amish passengers pointed out.

Buggies do not have seat belts—just thinly cushioned bench seats which provide more flexible seating and storage—but perhaps are not as comfortable as my sedan.

A few of my passengers asked me questions, mostly about why I was interested in the Amish. Many Amish women I met did not understand outsiders' persistent curiosity about their lifestyle, especially among visitors who unabashedly photograph their children.

"Imagine if we started taking photographs of English children without permission," one Amish woman said with a pinch of irritation in her voice.

The Amish refer to those who live outside their community as "the English," even those from foreign countries who do not speak English. But one pensive mother of six had another view about the perpetual interest in her Amish community.

"I would come visit, too," she said. "It is so beautiful where we live. I would be curious about people who live as we do."

Over the course of ten years, my Amish shopping companions introduced me to their family members, neighbors, and friends. Each patiently answered countless questions that I raised about their way of life.

With most of these women, my acquaintance remains at a polite distance. But with some, I have developed enduring friendships. We chuckle about sneaking healthier entrees into our evening meals, share concerns about our children, and trade family remedies for colds.

In the pages that follow, I have gathered reflections of my time spent with about two dozen Amish women in Lancaster County. My comments are not intended as generalizations about Amish women, either in Lancaster County or elsewhere. Rather, this book provides a glimpse into life in one Amish community as I experienced it, a life that generates as much curiosity as it does misinformation. I appreciate the accuracy of the expression "If you have met one Amish woman, then you have met one Amish woman." I have also learned that a well-ordered life of hard work and humility is anything but simple.

I am deeply grateful to those Amish women who have graciously accompanied me on innumerable shopping trips, shared meals with me, invited me into their homes and to their children's schools, and welcomed me to Amish gatherings. I hope I have been as respectful of their unfamiliar ways as they were about mine. Their companionship and friendship have been an unexpected gift and provided the context for this book.

Special Note: *In accordance with Amish modesty and convention, the names of individuals and their personal characteristics have been changed. Respecting and protecting the privacy of each woman and her family is of utmost importance.*

Call from Leah

LEAH WAS THE very last person I expected to telephone me on a Saturday evening after 10:00 p.m.

"I am sorry to call so late, but I can't find the road [on the map] where the Fisher family has moved. The Fishers are hosting church tomorrow. You are the only one I know to call at this hour."

Like all Amish women, my trim forty-year-old friend has never cut her chestnut-colored hair. With her part always pulled taut down the middle, two locks twisted at the crown, and hair bound tight at the nape of her neck, Leah is almost indistinguishable in a gathering of Amish mothers, each wearing the same head covering.

Leah, however, insists that she can easily identify one Amish woman from another even when they are not in clear view.

"I can usually tell by their horse and buggy," she once confided.

Through the phone, Leah sounded both panicked and apologetic.

"Do you know how to find Tabor Road? Can you use your computer to help me?"

If Leah telephoned her Amish neighbors at this late hour (or any hour), she could only leave a voicemail message. The Lancaster Amish use telephones but, as a rule, do not keep phones in their homes. Voicemail messaging has become more common among the Lancaster Amish, an accommodation to modernity made after much consideration from church leaders.

Asking me for help must have been a difficult decision for Leah, who is tenaciously self-reliant. Within her cloistered world, Leah handily tailors dresses for her five daughters and mends heavy coarse pants for her three sons and her husband. She prepares three meals a day for ten people, tends to eight children, ages one to twenty-three, and manages a thousand-pound horse and buggy with confidence. Over the summer, Leah gardens and preserves bushels of vegetables and fruits, enough to last the entire year.

DENNIS L. HUGHES

Telephoning an English woman who lives seventy-five miles away, for directions to an Amish neighbor whose new home is only a few miles down the road, took courage.

I shuddered picturing Leah inside the unheated wooden phone booth set back from the road, squinting at her creased map of Lancaster County, with a flashlight. It was a biting cold and howling, windy night.

Like many Lancaster Amish, Leah has a plastic push-button phone installed in a drafty wooden shed outside her home. The Amish selectively adapt to modern ways only after it has been demonstrated that the change will not erode the unity of their settlement. An Amish mother in her fifties remembers her lengthy waits for the one phone shared by several families when she was a girl. During the 1980s and 1990s, the church began permitting individual family phones but only outside the home. The Amish are late adapters to technology, if they adapt at all.[1]

As I searched for a detailed Lancaster County map on my laptop, I told Leah I would place her on speakerphone. Over time, Leah has learned that a computer can access directions to out-of-the-way destinations, though she is not curious about how the device works. Only when all other resources have been exhausted will Leah ask me for help via an internet search. Life is not expected to be easy for the Amish. Speed is not a virtue to be chased or valued. But on this night, Leah needed my assistance urgently.

I located the road in question. Google Maps only offers driving directions by car or by foot. I struggled describing suitable horse and buggy directions.

"Take Yost Road east heading toward Lapp Valley Farm. Tabor will be on the left, between New Hollander and Peters Road. If you get to Peters Road, you have driven too far."

Leah sent me a letter the following week:

"Greetings, Judy. Your directions to the Fishers worked well. They were so good, we had to slow down the horses for the last mile because we arrived much too early. Thank you!"

ONE

Getting to Know
the Amish

"WHY DO YOU live like that?" a European vendor asked an Amish woman purchasing a plant at the Philadelphia Flower Show.

"We were born that way," the good-natured Amish mother shrugged.

Amish Communities in the United States

The Amish began as a distinct group in 1525, their name taken from an Anabaptist leader named Jakob Ammann, who was born in Switzerland. Like other Anabaptist groups, the Amish believe that church membership—and along with it, baptism—should be a conscious choice made when one becomes an adult. In addition, Jakob Ammann stressed rigorous church discipline and separation from a world he viewed as full of temptation.[1] Ammann called for church members to avoid those who had committed an unrepented sin, a practice known as "shunning." With a view to instruct rather than punish, Ammann felt that shunning would encourage confession and repentance.

Fleeing religious persecution in Germany and Switzerland, the Amish arrived in America in the early part of the eighteenth century. Pennsylvania appealed to the Amish because of the commonwealth's reputation for religious tolerance, having previously welcomed the Quakers, Moravians, and Mennonites. The Amish eventually migrated to Lancaster County, rich in available farmland and reminiscent of the German and Swiss countryside.[2]

Today Lancaster County, Pennsylvania, hosts the largest Amish settlement in North America, with an estimated 41,795 Amish population recorded in 2021. The next largest Amish communities reside in Holmes County, Ohio, and in Elkhart and LaGrange Counties, Indiana. At the time of writing, the total Amish population in the United States for adults and children is estimated to be 355,660.[3]

The Amish speak, read, and write fluently in English, but Amish children learn Pennsylvania Dutch as their first primary language at home. Derived from a German dialect, "Pennsylvania Deutsche" (or Pennsylvania German) has gradually become known as Pennsylvania Dutch. Although Lancaster County tourist destinations promote Amish attractions with Dutch symbols like windmills and wooden shoes, the association between the Netherlands and the Amish exists solely for commercial purposes.

As Amish children grow older, they learn to read and sing old German verses in their church hymnals, and eventually the youngsters become trilingual in Pennsylvania Dutch, English, and old German.

A visitor to an Amish community might notice that very young Amish children often stare blankly at the English customers who initiate conversation. Toddlers may not understand the English pleasantries. And like any attentive parent, Amish mothers and fathers caution their children about strangers. Young children raised within an Amish settlement, especially one as large as in Lancaster County, may be unaccustomed to adults who do not resemble their parents or neighbors.

Since 1960, the Amish population has doubled about every twenty years. The growing population can be explained by two long-term trends: a high birth rate and a high retention rate. On average, Amish families in Lancaster County raise seven or eight children and most teens choose to remain among their Amish family and peers.

Connection to the Land

"One of the few things we can't grow is land," an older Amish grand-mother mused as we drove through a web of winding roads and well-tended Amish fields.

I had always assumed that the Lancaster Amish largely depended on farming for their livelihood. But the most current data reveals a different story. Because of the expense and scarcity of farmland, seeking employment off the farm has become a necessity in many Amish households. While the Amish maintain large gardens that feed their families, currently less than half of the Lancaster Amish earn their living from farming.[4]

A graying Amish mother of six reflected wistfully on her transition away from traditional farming upon her marriage:

"The farm means family to me, working together side by side. I knew my husband was not a farmer when I married him, but the transition from growing up on a farm to operating a farmers market stall has taken me a long time to get used to."

When there is not enough farmland to go around, Amish fathers and sons seek employment as close to home as possible—working with their hands in carpentry shops or at produce distributors, in machinery repair businesses, small manufacturing plants, or landscaping firms.

Amish men who work in construction might be placed in a temporary job site far from home. A non-Amish co-worker or a paid driver typically transports Amish employees so that they can join a work site too far away for a reasonable walk, scooter, or horse and buggy ride. Valued as steadfast and reliable employees, Amish men work amicably with both Amish and non-Amish employers.

Yet still, the desire for a relationship with the land permeates Amish life. While this sentiment may be slowly changing among the younger generation, the Amish maintain their inextricable bond to rural life no matter where they work.

One well-read Amish father described the connection to the land this way: "Even if we only have a garden [and not a farm] the ethos is still very rural. None of us live in the city, we live in a small towns or villages."

An entrepreneurial middle-aged Amish woman, whose husband works alongside her at an Amish dry goods shop, admitted, "My husband spends his one weekday off helping mow the lawns of other Amish farmers. That's how much he misses working the land."

Centrality of the Church Community

The Amish are, first and foremost, a religious community—a fact that may not be apparent when driving by picturesque Lancaster County farmsteads. When the Amish "go to church," they do not gather in towering structures beneath spires and stained-glass windows. Instead, a church member's home becomes the sacred space, with services held every other Sunday.

What is the religion of the Amish? The Amish practice orthodox Christianity and follow the teaching of Jesus. In practical terms, Amish daily life folds around a literal interpretation of the Bible. Leading a life of modesty, working industriously, being self-sufficient, and maintaining separateness from the world lies at the heart of Amish identity.

The Amish are Anabaptists, believing that baptism should be a voluntary adult decision. Adult baptism is a choice that each older teen or young adult makes prior to becoming an official church member. The Amish may not marry until they are baptized.

For over two hundred years, the Amish have followed an oral road map that governs their life, called the *Ordnung,* the German word for "order." The *Ordnung* regulates everything from transportation via horse and carriage to the granular details of hairstyles or the fabrics appropriate for women's clothing. As bound to these rules as they are to their faith, the Amish follow their church's *Ordnung* with unwavering conviction.

"The rules keep our culture from disappearing. The standards we set are for our own protection," one Amish grandmother cautioned.

The *Ordnung*'s interpretation varies slightly in geographically dispersed settlements. For instance, the shape of the women's head covering may change as one travels through the six hundred-plus Amish communities in the United States. But Amish women will always wear a covering in deference to their faith, even though its profile may change. The *Ordnung*'s basic tenets remain consistent regardless of the Amish community one visits: rejection of public electricity, wearing plain dress, completing formal education at eighth grade, and relinquishing individual freedoms for the sake of community.[5]

Tenets of Amish Life

The Amish live separate from the public utility grid, a nonnegotiable part of Amish life. Instead, large batteries tucked in wooden bases power pole lamps. Compact, battery-operated lights also help illuminate darkened rooms when hooked to a nail or standing on a table.

While forbidden from connecting to the public power supply, the Amish may use batteries, solar power, or generators when they operate home sewing machines, a room fan, or a kitchen blender. Amish homes do not use microwaves, toaster ovens, garbage disposals, or standard electric washing machines.

> **When the Amish** purchase a house from a non-Amish owner, the community expects the removal of electrical wiring to be completed within a year or so.

Maintaining separation from the electrical network restricts telephone access within the home. The Amish feel that phone calls interfere with the ebb and flow of family life and disturb hundreds of years of traditional communication by personal visits.

There are exceptions. One might notice Amish vendors at a farmers market with a cell phone or an Amish teen with a covert mobile device. One Amish parent noted that, over time, there has been erosion in his settlement around the parameters of phone and electrical use. Mobile phones have been a thorny issue in many Amish communities, creating tension about appropriate usage.

"Telephones bring the outside world in when it is not wanted. We would be on the phone too long if we spoke directly to one another. We use the phone to leave messages on important information, if someone got hurt, or if someone is in the hospital," one Amish mother pointed out.

Since phones are not permitted inside the home, the Amish construct sheds for their telephones, like the one from which Leah initiated her call to me. That shed can be stifling hot in the summer, bone-chilling cold in the winter, and deluged during rainstorms.

Voicemail in the Amish community has become more common. Collecting voicemail messages from the phone shanty requires leaving the house and darting outside multiple times a day.

The inconvenience of the phone keeps calls short and to the point. A small note pad and a couple of stubby pencils typically line the wooden shelf where the phone rests.

"Even if I could have a phone in my kitchen, I would not want one," said one Amish mother of seven. "I like to concentrate when I am peeling potatoes, and a phone call would interrupt that peace."

Values of Hard Work and Family

Amish family members often live near one another, and settlements encompass tight networks of both kin and long-time friends. Siblings walk to school together. Families attend church as a unit.

"Can all your seven children fit inside the buggy for a trip to church?" I asked a thick-waisted Amish mother.

"If they want a ride, they do," she laughed.

Shouldering hard work is another cornerstone of Amish life.

Whether one is young or old, physical labor goes hand in hand with being Amish. The biblical idea that man should "live by the sweat of his brow" (found in Genesis 3:19) plays a pivotal role in leading a pious Amish life. Learning the value of hard work starts as early as possible in Amish households.

Fulfilling one's obligations to the family is an expectation from a child's earliest years and is reinforced daily. As they grow up, daughters and sons assume more adult duties benefitting their household and their community. With families of seven or eight children and two adults, tackling household chores demands dutiful attention. Leisure time remains limited.

I received this letter from an Amish mother updating me on her family's weekend activities:

> Yesterday, we had a fun family workday. The girls and I cleaned the yard of leaves, Michael and the boys cleaned out the horse stalls. Caroline is washing dishes and Miriam is doing the rinsing. David is done with clearing off the table and now he is reading a farm magazine. Dad is doing his book work. I want to stir together some cookies and sew pants—I cut two pair yesterday and would like to have those done by tonight. Time for bed. May God Bless you!

Amish women command a valued role that revolves around their family and their home, performing tasks that require patience and persistence. Caring for multiple children, managing daily household routines, sewing clothes for each family member, preparing, preserving, and storing food, cooking meals for a large brood—each completed without the conveniences of modern life.

"I fear that someday there will be a half hour with nothing to do," exclaimed a mother with seven children.

Being stretched in several directions simultaneously seems like the sweet spot for the Amish women I met. Some Amish mothers extend their traditional roles by hosting multicourse suppers for tourists in their kitchens or basements, supplementing their household's income.

Selling homemade preserves, baked goods, crafts, or produce from a small stand or shop next to

> **I met a woman** who stitches together the heavy black suit coats worn by Amish men on church Sundays and reverential occasions. While those coats seem rudimentary to an outsider, closer examination reveals well-hidden hooks and eyes embedded into the inner lining that fastens the coat together along with intricate tailoring.

JUDY STAVISKY

Crimping the folds and stitching an Amish covering (or Kapp) requires a deftly skilled seamstress.

their home provides women with another opportunity for additional income. A handful of women specialize in sewing the delicate head coverings worn every day by Amish women. In general, if there are young children in the home, Amish mothers limit their outside employment and focus on their hefty responsibilities at home.

Accommodation to Modern Life

Despite their iron-clad prohibition against owning or driving a car, the Amish sit comfortably as passengers in a car or van (except for a small conservative minority). While child restraint or booster seats are not used in Amish buggies, the Amish understand safety seat requirements in English automobiles. In fact, the Amish families I met owned at least one child car seat.

Typically, the Amish use their horse and buggy when driving distances within five miles of their homes. Non-Amish retirees, people

JUDY S'AVISKY

Find the right farm and the suit maker
will assure a proper fitting.

between jobs, and those needing a little extra cash provide car or van service for the Amish. "Amish taxis" as they are called (though lacking taxicab markings) charge one dollar or more per mile plus waiting time, making outings beyond the immediate Amish community an expensive undertaking. Amish women must carefully map out their outings if their journey requires a paid driver.

"We have a list of drivers, but they can be busy two weeks in advance. If you need a last-minute ride, you could call your entire list of drivers and still not find someone available to take you," affirmed one mother of eight. "I never know who to call first when I need to make a doctor's appointment, the doctor or the driver. It can cause a great deal of stress."

By necessity, Amish women must be prudent planners, avoiding last-minute arrangements whenever possible.

TWO

Church as Foundation

Amish Church

"You might be able to live without your family. But you cannot live without your church," a mother in her thirties told me emphatically.

In lieu of a freestanding building, the Amish meet in a church member's home every other Sunday. Gathering in a neighbor's house or outbuilding underscores the intimate connection between religious and family life.

The church community serves as a spiritual anchor and much more. Steadfast reliance on one another in joyful and troubled times binds church families to each other. Members depend upon each one another for solace, fellowship, and strength.

When a serious illness or tragedy strikes an Amish family, the "church ladies"—women and girls from the congregation—will take on the incapacitated wife's daily responsibilities. Oven-warm meals arrive in abundance. Tag teams of mothers and daughters load the family's laundry into the wringer washer and hang the garments on the outside clothesline. In the case of an injured husband, the men of the congregation, often laden with tool belts, undertake the heavy chores, attend to the horses, and make repairs where needed.

In Lancaster County, twenty to forty families living in proximity to one another make up a church district.[1] Given the size of Amish families, church membership can range from one hundred to one hundred thirty people. When the number of family members exceeds the ability to comfortably fit inside a typical Amish home, basement, or barn, the church will split into two districts.

Unmarked church borders can be as subtle as "south of the old apple orchard" or "on the east side of Leacock Road." Even so, members can accurately map their church's geographic parameters. Families do not have the option of joining another church district unless they transplant their family to a different location, beyond their district's boundaries.

"Those boundaries are set in stone," an Amish grandmother informed me.

The Amish do not encourage dissension or disputes with the ministers' directives or their biblical interpretations. On occasion, an Amish father may question or even disagree with his church's interpretations of the *Ordnung*. But if the conflict persists over time, he and his family will move their home and possessions into a church district where the rules feel more compatible.

"When the church makes a rule, it is our obligation to follow," the same grandmother confirmed.

Home as a Sanctuary

"We don't have a church building. So, each family that can manage it will host church once or twice a year. Every family takes a turn. By holding church every other week in someone's home, we share the honor and the work," an Amish mother of six elaborated. Church services typically last three hours.

If an expectant mother finds that her family's church date conflicts with her newborn's arrival, she will change her hosting date with another family. Switching dates with other families may require a dozen phone calls (remember, phone calls immediately go into voicemail). But eventually, another family exchanges their church date.

Welcoming the church membership into one's home guides the construction and renovation of Amish homesteads. In some Amish houses, partitions that resemble walls can be removed, creating one open space accommodating scores of church members on a given Sunday.

Other families build a separate structure, sometimes adjacent to or on top of the horse barn, for the purpose of hosting church, large youth group gatherings, and family reunions.

Uninsulated barns and cold basements can be chilly sanctuaries during the winter, even when supplied with propane heaters. In such circumstances, church members with spacious unheated areas might swap their church day with a family whose interior space provides more warmth.

Amish families with more confined home interiors might use their barn (in the summer) or their basement when hosting church. Newlyweds will host church once they feel settled and have sufficient space to do so. Churches excuse elderly couples from

> The church rules permit propane heaters in the winter. Box fans are not used during summer church services, regardless of the temperature.

hosting church, especially if all their children—who would help them make church preparations—have married and live away from home.

"There is nothing that cleans a house like company coming," one good-humored Amish mother affirmed.

Hosting church requires several weeks of scrupulous sweeping, scrubbing, and mopping. Transforming one's home into a sacred space depends on the entire family laboring together. The date scheduled for hosting church looms large among Amish families.

I have visited with several Amish women in the weeks prior to their assigned church date. In the spring and summer, older children power-wash the picket fences; younger children mulch the flower beds; mothers spritz and wipe the windows inside and out until they gleam. Fathers and sons repair building structures and fences, scrub the barn windows, repoint crumbling stone walls, and apply a fresh coat of paint here and there. Horse stalls, while always kept clean, will be swept extra carefully.

"No one will probably notice those barn windows, but I'll know they are clean," a reticent Amish woman whispered to me.

Mopping the linoleum floors until they shine and polishing worn woodwork to a brilliant luster transforms a humble home into a house of worship. Detailed attention to each task contributes to a revered family ritual: family members (and assorted relatives) laboring together as they prepare for their church meeting date.

"There is much joy in shared work," one Amish grandmother reminded me.

In the winter, families hosting church shovel the snow before the early morning arrivals and find space for at least two dozen horses and as many parked buggies. The water trough for the horses must be free of dirt and unfrozen. Providing fresh hay for the church members' horses remains a responsibility for each season at church.

The eldest girl in one Amish household instructed me on the specific steps required as she and her siblings launched their meticulous cleaning projects.

"First, we mop all the ceilings. Then we scrub the walls. Closets get sorted and cupboards straightened. We take down the window shades and wipe both sides. The stove is the hardest job, but I really don't mind cleaning it," she assured me.

At fourteen years old, she had memorized the process required for hosting church and eagerly joined her family's flurry of sprucing up activities.

"I look forward to hosting church," her mother exclaimed. "And I will be glad when all this cleaning is behind me!"

Hosting Church

"I am sure we do things that others think are unusual," said one Amish woman. This is certainly true when it comes to the methodical preparation for hosting church. Each church district owns a "bench wagon," an enclosed cargo carrier that arrives at the host family's home a few days before the service, usually delivered by a team of horses. The bench wagon contains every item, except food, required for a church gathering of over one hundred people.

As the carrier's name implies, long wooden church benches rest on racks that line the inside of the bench wagon. The number stenciled on one end of the bench indicates its length. The adjoining black letters represent the initials of the church district to which the bench belongs. The utilitarian seating will be arranged neatly around the designated area and provide seating for the church service.

Amish church seating stacked
meticulously in the bench wagon.

JUDY STAVISKY

Each compartment of the bench wagon has a label that details
the items within, for example, "Front Right Hand Compartment
Contents— twenty-six regular folding chairs, four folding chairs with
armrests, one pie safe." Plates, cups, and assorted cutlery have been
carefully counted and repacked by the previous host family and found
in a nearby nook. The host family will also find enough hymnals for the
entire congregation, stacked in another bench wagon cubby.

Even though church services do not commence until 8:00 a.m., con-
gregants and extended family members begin arriving well beforehand.
Early-arriving men and boys huddle together, either outside in better
weather or inside the barn on colder days. The women and girls gather
in the kitchen, helping with last-minute food prep and catching up
with one another before the service begins.

After a bit of visiting, church members line up outside, split into
two queues by gender and then by chronological age, oldest to youngest. Lining up and entering the sacred space with solemnity and deference to one another is part of Amish church custom. Church services
begin promptly.

The predictable flow and slow pace of church helps secure the
Amish way of life, firmly rooted in the past. The longest tenured ministers enter the space first, followed by those more recently ordained.

The ministers settle into folding chairs, a slight nod to the marginal comfort earned as a servant leader.

The hosting couple ushers in the two lines of church members, separated by gender. Depending on the meeting space and the number of entrances, the eldest married men or women enter without a word, oldest to youngest. Elderly or frail members may select one of the extra folding chairs.

> **Tradition dictates** the order in which members enter an Amish church service, a pattern repeated every other week for hundreds of years.

In descending chronological age order, the single men (or women) file in next. If the men are seated first, the hosting wife will then usher in the married women (including widows) and seat them oldest to youngest. Young unmarried women follow those who are married or widowed. The youngest girls enter last, again seated according to birth order. Girls and boys under age nine will sit alongside their fathers or mothers.

Single men and women in their thirties have the option of sitting with either married or single members. As most of the other singles are teens or in their twenties, the older singles often join the married men and women of a similar age. In some communities, pregnant women may be offered a chair during the service instead of a bench seat.

"Benuel will be nine next week," his sister announced. "He will be able to enter church with the older boys."

Turning nine may be just another birthday to non-Amish children. But for Amish boys and girls, turning nine signals a leap toward adulthood. Instead of entering church as a little kid alongside their parents, a nine-year-old earns a much-anticipated seat between their peers with proximate birthdays.

DONALD REESE

An Amish family walks to church.

Still, it takes concerted self-discipline not to giggle or fidget during the service at nine years old. The bench seat next to a parent remains available to noncompliant children, an undesirable spot for a nine-year-old who has earned a sliver of independence.

"I am used to the long service. We get to sit next to our friends. We are not supposed to whisper, not even just a little. We look forward to the weeks when we go to church," said the daughter of one of my Amish companions.

Chances are, if a member remains in one church district throughout their lifetime as many do, they will sit side by side or near the same two people from childhood through adulthood. This ingrained order and repetition of routines helps create the bedrock of Amish life. Young church members who share decades sitting together through hundreds of church sermons often become life-long friends.

"I was named after Barbara. My mother sat next to Barbara until she moved away to get married. And I get a birthday card from Barbara every year," an Amish teenager shared.

─◦◦───

The church service starts with the congregation singing an opening hymn, followed by a short sermon, Bible readings, and then a lengthy sermon of about an hour followed by more hymns. An Amish service does not include musical instruments, though the slow hymns have a lyrical quality to them.

A great grandmother added, "It is extremely rare for someone to miss church, even if they are feeling poorly, but the benches seem to get harder as we get older!"

Young children may bring a simple toy to the service, or a small plastic bag filled with a snack.

"My youngest often falls asleep during the church service, that way it goes by faster and she knows she can play with her friends afterwards," one mother reported.

Having participated in the church service since infancy, young children understand their parents' and the church's behavioral expectations during the three-hour service.

"Parents think about how the children will behave in church and in school. That's an extra incentive to keep the children in line at home," reaffirmed one mother.

Adults and children take bathroom and water breaks during the service. Mothers and newborns typically return to church when the baby is about six weeks old, and nursing mothers move

Bishops, ministers, and deacons assume their positions for life. Both a somber and momentous occasion, the choosing of a new bishop, minister, or deacon culminates in an event that swirls with apprehension and emotion. This lifetime post imposes substantial responsibilities on the man selected as well as his family.

to another part of the house when breastfeeding or calming a fussy baby. Aunts and grandmothers offer comforting arms and laps when crying infants need additional soothing.

Ministers for Life

"Some ministers are better speakers than others. Some get better as they age," pointed out one Amish grandmother, a woman who had attended more than fifteen hundred church services in her lifetime.

In general, the Amish have two ministers and one deacon for each church district and one bishop per two church districts.

"Church members will think about which man could best guide us," a younger mother elaborated. "We also try to consider other things like their current job and if they have small children at home. This is a life-long commitment and one that the family must assume as well."

All nominations remain strictly confidential. Church members do not know whom others may have nominated. Even married couple may not reveal their nominations to one another. The selection of a minister is considered sacrosanct.

While women have equal voting privileges, only men may be selected as servant leaders. The minister, charged with preaching the word of the Lord, does so largely through his sermons. The deacon administers the alms fund, making sure widows and the poor are provided for, and he assists in communion and baptisms. Deacons do not preach but are called upon to read scripture between sermons.

To select the next servant leader, each church member nominates the married man with the leadership qualities their church community requires. Those who receive at least three nominations will be included in "the lot."

After the nomination process, the men chosen for the lot will be seated around a table. Each will choose a hymnal and lay it in front of him. One of those books conceals a slip of paper. The slip of paper contains the verse (in German), "Into this lap the lot is cast but the fall is of the Lord" (Proverbs 16:33).

The man who unknowingly chose the hymnal with the hidden strip of paper will become the next minister of his church for as long as he maintains a capable mind and body. One of the bishops announces the chosen man's name. That man stands. With all hearts pounding, the bishop reads the ordination charge. Guided by divine intervention, the Amish feel that God has directed them in the choice of the best man for the job.

Without the benefit of theological training or additional salary, the new minister willingly accepts the daunting responsibility. The chosen minister will prepare and deliver sermons to his congregation for as many years as he retains his health.

As a longstanding Amish custom, ministers do not use written notes as guides for their sermons. The newly appointed minister has about six months before he will present his first hour-long sermon.

"It is a position that comes with obligations. There is much to get used to," explained one minister's wife of many years.

Ministers' families set an example of piety. There is a subtle understanding among the church membership that the minister, his spouse, and his children will embrace an even stricter code of appropriate behavior—dressing a little more conservatively, adhering more closely to Amish customs.

The minister's wife accepts her informal role as counselor to other church women. Reflecting her new status and tradition, the wife of the minister wears good Sunday footwear with a slightly higher top of her shoe.

"Not as comfortable as our regular good shoes," another minister's wife and mother admitted, greatly relieved when she unties her laces upon returning home from church.

Feeding the Faithful

"When you host church, everyone is in your kitchen," declared an Amish mother with a spirited personality.

In the weeks prior to the assigned hosting date, multiple church ladies offer their assistance with the food preparation for the one hundred-plus membership. The bond of mutual aid and support among the Amish builds on their deep sense of community, as they rely on one another without being asked.

"It is always the same meal, so it is easy to assign dishes when the church ladies call to help," said a mother of eight who was hosting church the following month.

Serving the same meal reaffirms the traditions and tamps down on prideful competition.

After the service, the men reassemble the benches, secure them with a wooden trestle, and create long sturdy tables and seating for the light meal served after the service.

The women lay plain tablecloths over the wooden tables and arrange place settings while lining the center of the tables with spongy loaves of homemade white and wheat breads, along with the traditional Amish church meal offerings.

The food served at the midday meal has varied little over the years. The church ladies find a space on the table for the two soft spreads traditionally served after every church service. One spread consists of

Benches secured by wooden
trestles become dining tables.

JUDY STAVISKY

melted American or Velveeta cheese folded into hot milk. Peanut butter whipped together with marshmallow fluff and corn syrup makes
another, sweeter spread. A popular Amish treat combines both these
toppings on one piece of bread.

Abundant bowls of garnet-colored pickled beets and crisp home-
cured cucumber pickles line the tables, each a staple of the church
meal. Butter and homemade jelly provide another familiar option.
Seasoned pretzels make their way onto many church tables as well.
Desserts include Snitz pie (composed of apple butter and apple sauce
baked in a pie shell), and every now and then another type of pie.

"It is nice to know what we will be eating and that this has been the
same meal for generations," one grandmother said.

Last summer, this grandmother's eldest daughter offered water-
melon for a church meal dessert when melon was ripe and plentiful.
The grandmother was not pleased.

"It is the small changes here and there that will eventually wear
away our culture," she chided her adult daughter.

Change in Amish society remains incremental and intentional.

THREE

Growing up Amish Right from the Start

Infants and Children

"It's important that our youngest learn what's expected of them, right from the start," a slim Amish mother stressed.

This mother of seven reiterated her community's belief that "being Amish" begins at birth.

"Our babies learn that this is the way we dress," she continued, as she loosely tied a stiff navy-blue infant bonnet around the head of her sixteen-month-old daughter.

Beginning in infancy, the uniformity of dress reinforces humility, elevating community standards ahead of self-expression. Hewing to past traditions—nothing that calls attention to oneself and nothing fancy (or "worldly," as the Amish would say)—parameters around attire safeguard a sense of belonging.

"We tend not to expose much skin, even when it's warm," she reiterated on a scorching hot day.

In a less conservative family, newborns might be dressed in either off-the-rack baby clothes or traditional Amish garments. But as a member of a conservative Old Order Amish church, this Amish mother cuts her baby's dress pattern from the navy blue and chocolate brown remnants from her other daughter's plain dresses. Onesies might be worn under Amish clothes, but, in the more conservative families, infant garments mirror a smaller version of their older sibling's clothes.

"My favorite part of the summer was giving my little sister a bath," exclaimed one ten–year-old sister.

The Amish welcome newborns into the world with unbridled enthusiasm and affection. The community views multiple children as

DENNIS L. HUGHES

divine blessings. Young children, closely shadowing the adults in their life, demonstrate great affection for infants, cooing at them in a playful and patient manner.

I observed many instances where girls as young as six years old confidently hoisted an infant onto their hip and assumed the role of an older sibling.

As one Amish mother of six confided, "It is considered a tragedy in the Amish community [not being able to have children]. Couples will grieve their whole lives. All we talk about is our children!"

Rites of Passage

When a newborn arrives, creamy noodle casseroles, golden chicken pies, and gently used baby clothes appear from the far reaches of the church community. Amish relatives and neighbors routinely stop by and tidy up the house or wash dishes while the new mother naps.

"We have lots of help," one mother assured me. "And nearly everyone has family members living nearby."

Mutual aid—neighbors helping neighbors, church members reaching out to one another—bolsters every stage of Amish life. Offers of practical assistance surround each new mother. I met an unmarried Amish sister who quit her full-time teaching job for the sole purpose of providing her married and pregnant sister with support for her first newborn. That is not unusual. Teenaged relatives, thrilled with the idea of a new niece or cousin, consistently offer weekly housecleaning or babysitting duty in the first several months of a newborn's life.

"It's just what we do," responded the former teacher when I expressed surprise that she had given up her teaching post.

Naming a baby takes on critical importance in the Amish community. Newborns often inherit the name of a living relative or a beloved family friend, an honor that further binds the community together. Given the number of siblings, first and second cousins, aunts, and uncles in an Amish clan, family gatherings often include several members with the same first names. Nicknames emerge over time and help distinguish the multiple Michaels, Rachels, and Samuels from one another (e.g., Big Mike or Sister Rachel). Sometimes, children can be distinguished by their fathers (e.g., Ben's Katie) or adults by their spouses (Elam's Rebecca). In school, middle initials help distinguish one Naomi from another.

Little Amish girls often name their dolls after the family's recent newborn.

A tight weave of rituals, repeated in households throughout the Amish community, envelops the children with centuries-old traditions. Before a noon meal, I watched an Amish mother of five, fold her left hand over her baby's tiny fingers, communicating the solemnity of grace said before and after every meal. Over time, the youngest family members understand that sitting motionless during mealtime prayers, just as in church, requires discipline and self-control: no snickering allowed.

"If the child is not taught in the high chair that 'no' means 'no,' they will find it hard to learn later. Learning patience early on is a good thing, especially when you are Amish," affirmed one grandmother with nineteen grandchildren.

When an Amish father, most often seated at the head of the table, bows his head before a meal, the children immediately lower and close their eyes, suspending all movement for a silent grace that can last two or three minutes.

The silent prayer ends when the father makes a slight gesture, like moving his chair or clearing his throat. After family members have completed their meal, they bow their heads once again, offering more silent gratitude before the children may clear the table.

In case of a father's absence, a mother leads the silent grace.

Speaking their own language, Pennsylvania Dutch, secures their privacy and further insulates the Amish from outside influences that could erode their way of life.

"The first language our children learn is Pennsylvania Dutch," several Amish mothers reminded me.

From the earliest years, Amish girls emulate their mothers and older sisters, sweeping, folding, and cleaning. The boys mimic the activities of their fathers and big brothers caring for the horses and completing barn chores. The completion of those daily tasks demonstrates to children the significance of their contributions to the household.

"There are always more chores for the children to do," I heard several mothers affirm with a laugh.

Younger children routinely scrape off bits of mud from "good Sunday shoes" onto old newspapers and polish the toe box to a shine. Four-year old girls eagerly try their hands at drying dishes with a makeshift stool pulled close to the sink. Older girls wash, rinse, and find places for the abundant stacks of plates and cutlery two or three times a day, scour the floors, mow the lawn, and move supplies from the cellar or outbuilding to the kitchen and back again.

While she mixes a meat loaf for supper or removes clothes from the lengthy laundry line, an older sister might also supervise her younger siblings folding piles of towels and rags.

"Be careful not to drag those clean things along the floor," an older sister warns, as she steps into the coveted role of mother.

Amish schoolchildren often face the early morning darkness as they begin their chores. Those who live on a farm help nurse a newborn calf or milk cows before the school day begins. Depending on the number of livestock that require attention, attending the dairy cows can take an hour or two *before* walking to school.

"The barn is cold, but the job goes faster when one of my brothers or sisters helps," notes a thirteen-year-old Amish girl who routinely assists with milking before school.

Scrapple, a Pennsylvania Dutch breakfast side dish, incorporates cornmeal mush and bits of pork scraps and trimmings, seasoned with spices and herbs. Often shaped into a loaf, sliced, and then pan fried, scrapple adds a savory touch to a breakfast plate.

Even in non-farm households, children's domestic chores can still take thirty minutes or longer before heading off to school. Without an electric dishwasher, cleaning dirty dishes, drying, and returning plates and glasses to the cupboard can be a cumbersome task with a family of eight or nine members. Scrubbing cornmeal mush, bits of sausage, bacon, or scrapple from encrusted pots requires a block of time and concentration.

As one mother offered, "Children grow into chores as soon as they are capable."

A longing for more difficult assignments encourages proficiency in simpler tasks fulfilled by the youngest children. Folding mounds of clean towels prepares little girls for the more complicated chore of laundering and drying piles of dirty clothes. Raking the leaves will eventually prepare little boys for the front and back yards that need mowing with a manual push mower.

"We all need to work together to get things done," said the oldest daughter in one Amish family that operates a small shop from their home.

─⟋⟍⟍⟍─

Children experience their indispensable role in maintaining their family's home and well-being every day. The early years reinforce the importance of fulfilling obligations to other family members.

"Doing chores develops character and responsibility to others like nothing else can," avowed an Amish grandmother with thirty-three grandchildren. "Our children know what is expected of them and telling them to do something only needs to be heard the first time. . . well, that's the goal anyway," she conceded.

Another mother admitted, "We need to be creative to find enough tasks and be able to delegate them to the children. That is the only way they will learn responsibility."

She admitted, "I know one mother who makes up chores when she runs out of the ones she really needs done. I noticed her children were weeding around a fence post that wasn't even on her property!"

As opposed to each family member carving out their own daily path, cooperating as part of one unit defines Amish life, rooting a deeper sense of attachment to their family and their community.

I spent a few days helping Amish women and their children tidy up the homes of bachelor uncles or never-married elders. On our hands and knees, we scrubbed narrow steps, washed each window, wiped down sticky refrigerator shelves, and dusted curio cabinets.

─⟋⟍⟍⟍─

"Children learn to yield to their parents when they are young, and that is a good characteristic to have if you are Amish," the same Amish grandmother remarked during one shopping trip.

There is much at stake in being well-behaved and having an obedient child. Each child's personal behavior reflects on their family. Pride evokes a swift reproach.

Resisting the urge to boast about an athletic feat or a new possession is not any easier for an Amish child than it is for non-Amish youngsters. However, Amish adults and older siblings quickly identify and discourage self-important behaviors.

"That was prideful," an older sister chided her younger brother, as he showed off how well he could throw the ball.

And he sheepishly nodded his head in agreement with her.

As Amish children grow up, they bend to the strict and modest dress standards of their community.

Perusing gently used black athletic shoes with a fifteen-year-old Amish teen, she pointed out the appropriateness of each potential choice to me.

"This pair is not plain enough [white stitching], and that pair is too fancy [with immovable brand insignia]," she noted.

While expressing a unique personal style may be the desire of those living outside their settlement, Amish teens seek assimilation by blending into their crowd.

As if to underscore this point, an eighteen-year old Amish teen described the moss-colored fabric that she and her teenage girlfriends had selected, bought, and then sewed into new dresses. Their desire: to be mirror images of each other. On the agreed-upon Sunday, the girls appeared *en masse* at a youth gathering. Even those like me, standing far away, could see the verdant wave of young women descending over the ridge. And in doing so, they fortified a shared tradition of being more alike than different in clothing literally cut from the same cloth.

I joined two elderly Amish grandmothers for a springtime birthday lunch at a local pizza shop, managed by an Amish family. The older women were inseparable childhood friends but had not seen each other through the winter months. In making the arrangements for the meeting, they agreed on wearing the same plum-colored dress, an expression of their devotion to one another and their long friendship. Each beamed widely as they spotted their age-old confidant across the pizza parlor, wearing the exact same dress.

Their reunion lunch reminded me of a comment another Amish woman shared with me months earlier: "I am happy with limited choice. You know, there can be strength in sameness."

Transitions from School

Amish children end their Amish school training at eighth grade. From that time until they marry, the teens will remain at home under the supervision of their parents and other related adults. With the one-room schoolhouse days behind them, young teens take on more responsibilities inside and outside their household.

Under the tutelage of their mothers, teenage girls practice and eventually master stitching traditional Amish patterns for homemade aprons, dresses, shirts, and pants. The first sewing project for most young girls: piecing together the patches for a "comfort quilt."

Piles of knotted comfort quilts wait for shipment to needy families across the globe.

JUDY STAVISKY

"Even you could do that, Judy," teased one of younger children of an Amish friend.

"Comfort knotting" or "comfort quilting" begins when women sew remnants of mismatched fabric squares together, at home. At a future date, the women gather and "knot" the squares together. The Mennonite Central Committee, a worldwide relief organization, is often the recipient, and they in turn distribute the warm coverings globally.

As one woman joked about a recent gathering of quilters, "Our mouths move as fast as our needles."

Alongside their mothers, daughters knead tender bread dough or bake sweet fruit pies in the family's kitchen. Over time, the girls learn menu planning, wash daily piles of laundry and iron special Sunday clothes. Mothers may task older adolescent girls with some of the canning responsibilities, balancing the vinegar and sugar needed in pickled beets or measuring the right proportion of spices for curing gallons of cucumbers.

Amish neighbors routinely provide apprenticeships to Amish teenagers who have graduated from their one-room schoolhouse.

"Our children don't really need to look for work. People call us with jobs for our teens," confirmed one mother with a recent Amish school graduate.

The Amish believe that consistent engagement in productive work is essential to developing self-reliance. Members of the Amish community create paid opportunities for youth apprenticeships so that the cycle of challenging work and learning by experience continues a decades-old custom.

Recent female Amish school graduates might find themselves with babysitting opportunities, housecleaning jobs, gardening for elderly couples, or working for a commercial buggy tour enterprise. If the teens are older, they could join others their age weighing deli meats and cheeses at a farmers market stand or stocking shelves in an Amish grocery store a few days a week. Even so, Amish mothers depend on their daughters committing one or two days a week at home assisting with laundry, housecleaning, baking, and tending the family's garden.

Adolescent boys who live on farms accept more responsible jobs as they grow up, like driving the mule team or operating a rented front end loader around the farm. At fifteen years old, boys might be offered an apprenticeship in a nearby carpentry or metal shop, nursery, or farm supply store. As teenage sons grow older, local employers know Amish youth have on-the-job experience and will likely be reliable employees.

Rumspringa: *Teens through Adulthood*

"Only ten weekends away," grinned a fifteen-year-old, reminding me of his upcoming sixteenth birthday.

By the time an Amish teen reaches fifteen-and-a-half-year-old, they keep a fastidious accounting of the number of weekends until *Rumspringa,* which begins officially on a teen's sixteenth birthday. *Rumspringa* is a Pennsylvania Dutch term literally translated to "running around."

A much-misunderstood period of Amish life, television and other media have projected distorted images of Rumspringa. The popular press has focused on a smattering of wild parties and inaccurate Amish "reality shows" that spotlight teenage mayhem and substance abuse. In truth, the vast majority of Rumspringa adolescents attend Sunday singings and spirited coed volleyball games, content with mingling among their friends and former classmates.

Rumspringa provides teens with the opportunity to experience the wider world as the focus of their lives gradually moves away from their nuclear family and toward a network of friends. Rumspringa offers

Baptism is a momentous and hallowed event. Once baptized, members must conform to their church district's exacting Ordnung.

young people their first church-approved taste of freedom beyond the rigid parameters of their Amish family. During this time, teenage Amish boys may hide a radio or a CD player below the dashboard of their buggy and listen to music, against the rules after baptism into the Amish church. A group of Amish teens may take in a Christian-themed movie or even purchase an iPhone, neither of which will be permitted after their adult baptism when they formally join the church.

The popularity of fictitious television series about the Amish contributes to the misperception that Amish adolescents flee their communities on the eve of their sixteenth birthday. In fact, the opposite is true. Data collected by the Young Center for Anabaptist Studies at Elizabethtown College in Lancaster County points out that about 85 percent of Amish young adults choose to become part of the Amish community through a formal baptism ceremony that typically takes place in their late teens or early twenties.[1]

Living among families that dress alike and eschew modern conveniences builds enduring personal connections. Sharing similar schooling, work ethic, and traditions establishes an unbreakable bond. The ebb and flow of Amish life anchors the only existence the teens have ever known.

Teenage friendship networks, evolved over years of socializing within the same church or Rumspringa group, buffer Amish adolescents from the outside world. Amish teens move effortlessly between two languages, English and Pennsylvania Dutch. Being raised in an Amish community creates familiarity, predictability, and deep friendships. For the majority of Rumspringa youth, leaving the comforts of a

I was woefully lost one day, driving with an Amish mother and two of her teenaged daughters to a remote fabric warehouse. My iPhone GPS coordinates were jumbled. One of my teenage passengers asked if she might input our destination. A few seconds later, she rekeyed the correct coordinates, and we were on our way.

stable devout community in pursuit of an unknown and foreign world is not a reasonable choice.

Amish teens tend to stay for other reasons, too. Graduating with only an eighth-grade education precludes Amish teens from obtaining most jobs outside their community. Jobs beyond the Amish settlement generally require a high school degree or its equivalent. Most Amish teens seem content with the nearby Amish and non-Amish employers that provide apprenticeships and hire Amish teens once they reach legal working age, even without a high school degree.

For the first time in their lives, Rumspringa allows Amish teens an opportunity to participate in large peer group activities, independent of their parents, though still under the eyes of watchful adults. The youth groups (or "gangs" as the Amish refer to them) meet up at least once or twice a week with additional gatherings organized in the fine weather. A few adults are always present.

If they can afford it, Amish families purchase a horse and buggy for their sons when they turn sixteen. A horse can cost anywhere from five thousand to eight thousand dollars, and a pre-owned buggy around six thousand dollars. A new buggy may cost twice as much. When a family has several boys aged sixteen and older, vehicle acquisition can be an expensive proposition. The eldest boy might receive a horse and carriage and share it with the next eldest son. Logistics are less complicated if all the siblings join the same youth group.

Determining which gang will be the best fit is a critical decision in an Amish teenager's life, one made in heavy consultation with parents. Parents weigh youth group options assiduously, particularly for their eldest teen. Often younger siblings will follow their brothers and sisters and join the same group, though that is not required. The selection of Rumspringa group circumscribes the choice of a marriage partner and draws a dotted line around a teen's immediate and future friendship circles. Parents keep a close eye on the reputation of the youth group and how it may evolve over time.

Like non-Amish mothers and fathers, Amish parents hope that their teens will select a group with a good reputation. For instance, different Amish youth groups will provide more or less restrictive dress code requirements for their members. This might explain a teenage Amish boy wearing a faded English tee-shirt under his traditional suspenders and broadfall pants. Multicolored socks peeking over the top of a teenaged girl's black athletic shoes could be a sign that a teen is headlong into

Teens enjoying the company of one another.

Rumspringa, belonging to a youth group that permits leniency with clothing choices.

Rumspringa teens have a bit wider swath of independence and may reexamine the strictures of Amish life. But not every teenage gesture in Rumspringa becomes one of open defiance or rebellion. I have noticed an extra decorative button on the sleeves of teenaged girls and shaggier than usual haircuts on young men in Rumspringa, signaling a slight move away from uniformity, but still within the traditional structures that have governed their lives thus far.

As one parent said, "We would prefer that teens not test the boundaries of Amish life, and we know it will happen."

But this is the time to do it; once a teen becomes a baptized member of the Amish church, another layer of accountability will be imposed.

Each Rumspringa youth group has a name such as the Eagles, the Meadowlarks, the Lariats (a rope or cord used with horses or cattle). Gangs typically cover a specific geographic area, though teens may join a gathering other than the one in closest proximity. Youth groups can swell up to one hundred teens. When membership becomes too large, the group will split and spin off into two groups.

One parent noted that while having the teens join a youth group closer to home may be preferable, "You can't divide up the youths' hearts and friendships with roads."

Some youth groups circulate a printed list of gatherings for upcoming months (copied by one of the schoolteachers or fathers working in a shop with a photocopier). Groups might go fishing, play baseball or volleyball, and ice skate in the winter. Teens frequently post these lists on their home refrigerator door.

> **At the first sign of frost,** Amish teens drop off their skates for sharpening at the local shoe store. Ice skating is a favored sport by children, teens, and Amish adults.

Adolescent young men may be embarrassed riding to youth events in the family's stodgy buggy with a slow horse. Like their English counterparts, teens much prefer a snappier coupe, a "courting buggy," which is completely open, faster, and has a bench seat for two riders.

Other groups communicate by a phone chain, leaving detailed voicemail messages for one another with the time and place of the next scheduled event. Word of mouth between teens is an equally reliable method for communicating planned youth activities.

Each gang member's family takes a turn hosting the youth, typically once or twice a year. Circulating the hosting schedule well in advance allows time to prepare for the onslaught of teens. The host family provides snacks, supper, and beverages as well as a space for the singing and an area to socialize. Reflecting their traditional values, the Rumspringa men pick up the young women who need a ride to the youth event. I

DENNIS L. HUGHES

learned that Amish girls feel comfortable contacting a boy from their youth group and requesting a ride to a youth gathering.

"The English think we save money by not having a car, but we don't," chortled an Amish father with three teenage boys. He continued, "Our [older] teenaged children are busy many nights. If the activity is close by, our youth will drive the horse and buggy. But often, if the event is far away, we hire a driver to take them and bring them home. It gets awfully expensive!"

After church on a Sunday and on non-church Sundays, the youth congregate at the designated home in the late afternoon. Weather permitting, the teens relish vigorous games of volleyball on coed teams.

> **Youth group** geographic boundaries do not always match the church district parameters. A mother might host church one Sunday morning for one hundred-plus church members and then welcome another hundred teens that same evening, drawing guests from two adjacent regions.

Some barns or basements can comfortably accommodate other types of group games in inclement weather. When battering rainstorms make it impossible for volleyball outside, teens will bring their own board games for inside entertainment.

Those families with two or three teenagers in the same youth group will host the gatherings multiple times a year.

Many families host both church and their teens' youth group on the same day.

"The house is already clean. This way, all the work is completed at once," many Amish mothers insisted.

After several rousing sets of volleyball (or indoor games during inclement weather), the host family and a few volunteer moms load platters of food onto movable tables. Menus might include homemade pizza, a potful of beef chili or chicken corn soup, a platter of crisp salad with ranch salad dressing (always ranch dressing), pretzels, and chips. Teenaged girls demonstrate their culinary skills in a subtle way by providing an array of homemade desserts. I grocery shopped with one teen who detailed how she hid bite-sized Hershey's chocolate kisses in her cupcake molds, updating the traditional recipes with a touch of whimsy.

> **Recipe for Meadow Tea:** Boil a big pot of water, at least a gallon. Remove from heat and add a few handfuls of fresh mint. Add a cup of sugar and stir. Strain mint leaves out and serve.

On steamy hot days, boys with sweat-soaked hair plastered to their foreheads dig out a comb from their pants pocket and freshen up after a heated volleyball game and before the communal meal. Waiting for their turn in front of the small mirror hung near the host's kitchen, the girls readjust their head coverings and pin back loose strands of hair. Even though teens want to look their best to members of the

opposite sex, Amish culture shuns vanity. Small mirrors in the front room help maintain humility.

As the boys lope to the supper table and heap food onto their plates, the girls queue for their supper on the opposite side. Each teen balances a thin paper plate with familiar foods and plastic cutlery along with a disposable cup filled with water, meadow tea, or pre-packaged instant lemonade. Some beverages are not worth making from scratch for a hundred teenagers.

For the most part, the youth gobble down their meal then chat, bunched together with their own gender groups. A few days before the sing, the community's bench wagon had delivered seating to the host's property. Parents spread out the benches and hymnals in the barn space or basement in advance of the youth's arrival.

A handful of Amish adults attend the singing along with the host's parents and other relatives. Before the singing begins, the youth enter the area with the arranged benches and shake the hands of all the grown-ups sitting on the perimeter (including the non-Amish adults)—a sign of respect for those attending.

The youth pick up the hymnals at the end of each bench that provide the songs for the evening singing. The girls settle in on one side of the room, and the boys make their way onto the benches on the opposite side. Sitting at the center of the large gathering, the teenage host, surrounded by his or her closest friends (both girls and boys), starts by calling out the page numbers of selected hymns. German hymns are common, but a few have English verses. As the dulcet teenage voices blend in unison, an outsider forgets about the lack of a guitar or keyboard in the background. Except for a harmonica for personal use, the Amish I met did not use any musical instruments.

The singing lasts about an hour. I noticed some of the boys fidgeting, impatient for the last hymn. The real socializing begins after the singing. Organized again on long tables, bowls of chips, popcorn, cookies, and cups of water fortify the teens for the remainder of the evening. Now, the youth break up into smaller groups, young men mixing with the young women. After graduating eighth grade, Amish youth have few other opportunities for face-to-face interaction with their friends, and the *Youngie* (the Amish term describing youth group participants) cherish these gatherings.

Clumps of teens, chums since childhood, find easy fellowship with one another. A handful of youth might mix it up a bit, introducing themselves to newcomers. A few older boys with more targeted romantic intentions may train their attention on a particular young woman. Typically, the teens socialize in small groups late into the evening. Upon their departure, each teen shakes the hand of the other attendees. Struggling to remain alert the following Monday is an inevitable consequence of late night Rumspringa Sundays.

> **Budding Amish** teen romances often commence and continue with handwritten correspondence.

"If we are just working at home the day after a late youth group, Mom lets us sleep in, just a little," an older teen disclosed.

The young adults will travel a significant distance to the youth group that they (and their parents) determine to be a suitable match. A challenge unfolds when a member of the youth group meets a potential partner who lives a significant distance away. That makes dating more complicated. A horse tethered to a carriage can only travel so far in a day.

Rumspringa activities are not confined to weekend socials. In less restrictive youth groups, a cluster of same-sex teenagers in their late teens and early twenties might rent a beach house or a cabin in the Pocono Mountains for a few days over the summer. Others might venture on a weeks-long United States cross-country tour with teens from other

Plain communities (like Mennonite youth) closely supervised by adult chaperones. But many Rumspringa teens find contentment staying close to home and participating in the many activities scheduled for young people their own age within their immediate community.

Amish teens typically live in their parents' home until they are married. The Amish marry earlier than the English—early to mid-twenties for young women and men. According to the U.S. Census Bureau in 2021, the estimated median age for first-time American marriages was 28.6 for women and 30.4 for men.[2]

Participation in youth group activities cements life-long friendships. I met several married Amish women who not only met their spouse in their youth group but also maintain relationships with other couples from their former gang. Adults who continue their friendship network from their youth group are referred to as a "buddy group." If an adult maintains a close connection with a particular friend from their youth group, they are known as their "sidekick." There is an exceptional bond between married adults and members of their original youth groups. Some couples continue to have periodic gatherings long after marriage, children, grandchildren, and great-grandchildren.

In late October, a jubilant Amish mother shared that "We have six weddings to attend in the next eight days. There will be many friends from our youth group we haven't seen in years."

"Weddings are important in our community. We need to be there," reiterated another Amish mother, who was planning on attending eight wedding in as many days.

Amish weddings in Lancaster County are commonly held from the end of October through early spring, mostly on Tuesdays and Thursdays, starting at 8:00 am and ending late in the evening.

FOUR

All in a Day's Work

"Front doors are only for salesmen,"
conceded one Amish woman.

Hearth and Home

While Amish homes have easily accessible front doors, most visitors
find their welcome through the kitchen, located in the back or on the
side of the house.

As I drove down country roads in search of shopping companions'
addresses, I was struck by the number of contemporary Amish houses
in northern Lancaster County. A modern custom-built house at the
end of an unpaved driveway was as likely to be an Amish home as a
traditional farmhouse with a porch and gabled roof.

As Amish families expand and their children marry, new home construction and divided lots follow. While remaining near family and kin

remains a high priority among the Amish, young families will move to other rural communities in search of affordable land.

In Lancaster County, Amish homes come in a variety of styles, but their interiors remain strikingly similar. Spacious Amish kitchens meld into the living area, serving as the central hearth of the home. Amish kitchens embody a "living room" in the literal sense of the words: the hub of family devotional prayers, communal meals, and a space where family members share the day's events, write letters, read, and visit with neighbors.

Plain Formica kitchen counters typically wrap around two or three spacious walls in Amish kitchens. While the English decorate their kitchens with canisters of colorful dried beans and crocks stuffed with cooking utensils, few rustic décor elements embellish Amish kitchens.

Built for function and utility, Amish home kitchens facilitate the preparation of nearly two hundred individual meals a week (for a family of eight or nine), all made from scratch. Room for kneading bread, cultivating yogurt, growing sprouts, canning and fermenting produce, and rolling out cookies and pie crusts requires serviceable space without unnecessary flourishes.

And when hosting church, another hundred-plus church members will be served in a single day, with the assistance of other Amish women.

A simple clock positioned near a complimentary calendar from Kauffman's Fruit Farm and Market might hang on one wall. A list of

Bread loaves must cool before being placed into plastic bags.

JUDY STAVISKY

family relations will be tacked up in a place where they can be read with ease. A washcloth-sized mirror hung inconspicuously at waist level, providing just enough reflection for a quick comb through tousled hair or

> **Whenever I see a mirror** in an Amish home, I think of a small poster I noticed in an Amish school: "What you do shows who you are."

straightening a covering gone awry. Neatness may be a virtue, but the Amish discourage prideful primping.

Families eat their meals around a long wooden table in the heart of the kitchen, usually covered by an unadorned tablecloth, sometimes mended or with a faint stain. Children set the table with shatterproof melamine plates and bowls. Drinking glasses suggest odds and ends of previous collections, often plastic or acrylic—the larger the family, the more mismatched glasses and dishes. A shopping trip to a Re-Uzit shop (local thrift store) on the outskirts of town provides replacement dishware and utensils at bargain prices.

Often a second sink rests just along the side of the kitchen so that the family members returning from barn chores can wash up there instead of sullying the dish basin.

Neutral-colored linoleum typically covers the kitchen floor and extends throughout Amish homes, including the bedrooms.

"It is easier to keep a linoleum floor clean, especially when your children are running in and out of the barn," maintained one slight Amish mother.

Amish homes do not have wall-to-wall carpeting, viewed as superfluous and too worldly.

"We don't need vacuum cleaners either," the same mother reminded me.

The Amish take pains avoiding being prideful in small and large ways. Their homes reflect that modesty and humility. Nothing "fancy," nothing that makes one stand out from the crowd.

"Simplicity brings satisfaction," an older Amish woman reminded me.

Instead of carpeting attached to the floor, the Amish I met use throw rugs that can be shaken outside or hung on a laundry line and cleaned with a good whack of a broom.

A durable sofa or two, a couple of well-used stuffed chairs, and a plain bookcase typically furnish the living area. Sometimes a fabric cover protects the seating from the wear and tear of energetic children.

A wooden and glass breakfront cabinet, common in Amish homes, protects cherished family heirlooms, teacups, and wedding china, seldom touched or used. A movable wooden lamp cabinet, hiding a battery within, provides a base for a pole light that helps brighten the room.

Homes have an assortment of religious books, Amish newsletters and bulletins, catalogues, and farm-related magazines arranged neatly in a rack or on the edge of a table. Since the Amish do not own televisions or radios, they have more time for perusing Amish publications and in some households, the local daily paper.

Green roller shades, in lieu of accordion-pleated blinds or curtains, cover the windows in Amish homes throughout Lancaster County. Occasionally an Amish family hangs a simple wall sign that says "Family" above a door transom or affixes a decal stating, "Love of a Family is Life's Greatest Blessing," reminders of core Amish values.

Nondescript living areas never exhibit collections of baby pictures or heirloom family photographs. The Amish believe that individuals posing for snapshots violate the biblical commandment, "Thou shalt not make unto thee any graven image." Posed photographic images show hubris and pride.

One of the exceptions to Amish utilitarian simplicity can be found in unusual wall clocks sold in a few Amish dry goods shops. At the top of the hour, the timepiece's face opens and reveals the interior mechanical gears and wheels. After exposing the clock's inner workings, the clock's dial returns to its customary position. These battery-operated timepieces also ring every sixty minutes with a stanza of Americana and folk melodies (e.g., "America the Beautiful" and "Greensleves").

Another type of Amish clock favored by teenage Amish boys, projects an auctioneer's rapid-fire bid calling at the top of the hour (in lieu of song). While the Amish prohibit listening to musical broadcasts on any device, families may allow a snippet of a song or the auctioneer's call within their home wall clock.

The same thinking applies to a child's artwork. Many Amish children enjoy drawing and coloring. But their sketches will not be taped to the refrigerator. The Amish frown upon calling attention to oneself. Placed in a drawer, children's artwork can be viewed when there is a reason to do so.

A cast iron coal stove, located in the open living area, warms both the kitchen and the family room to a cozy temperature. Piles of thick blankets and quilts compensate for the lack of heat in Amish bedrooms. Amish homes will not use central heating, deemed by many to be too worldly. From time to time, when illness strikes, family members will temporarily move a bed closer to the living room coal fire for rest and recovery.

After the supper dishes have been washed and put away, children and teen do not vanish into their bedrooms or sequester themselves in the basement playing video games. Instead, family members relax together in the warmer living room area. Children read, work on jigsaw puzzles, or help parents with outstanding chores. The older Rumspringa teens

Old-fashioned coal stoves are common in Amish homes.

JUDY STAVISKY

might attend a social event away from home. Fathers pay bills or finish up paperwork. Mothers use their evening time to catch up on sewing, baking, or letter writing, or to get a head start on school lunches for the following day.

The living room stove serves another important purpose—drying winter laundry. Washing and drying the family's clothes and linens is a perennial challenge, particularly on drizzly days or during long stretches of sunless winter weeks. The Amish rarely use gas clothes dryers, deemed too extravagant and expensive. Damp towels and heavy socks draped over collapsible wooden drying racks become living room fixtures in the winter, nestled close to the coal stove.

Whenever I purchase a small gift for an Amish child, they immediately offer to share it with their siblings, even on their birthday (though occasionally Mom might need to remind them).

Privacy remains elusive in Amish homes. Children generally share bedrooms with at least one or more siblings. When space is tight, the younger same-sex children may share a bed. Sharing space, toys, and other possessions marks a deeply ingrained value, one that parents cultivate early and weave into every part of Amish life.

Laundry

"Amish women are always doing laundry," concluded one jovial Amish father of six.

Keeping up with laundry for an average family of nine or ten requires a vigorous effort, most often undertaken by the household's women. Retired men might help their elderly wives, but clothes washing is the task of mothers and daughters, with assistance from sons upon request.

> **Without a radio or cell phone**, Amish women are mindful about the weather. An unexpected rainstorm could ruin hours of work invested in washing and drying the family's laundry.

Amish families depend upon old-fashioned wringer washers, like the ones most Americans used until the early 1950s. While some Amish use spinners (reconditioned washers that only spin the laundry), clothes dryers are uncommon, and considered worldly and expensive.

DENNIS L. HUGHES

"With nine people in my family wearing at least two outfits a day and sometimes three [for work or school, for home chores, and for a youth event], we need to do laundry almost every day just to keep up," an Amish woman admitted good-naturedly.

Operating a wringer washer demands physical labor, a keen sense of organization, and a block of time every single day, except Sunday, a day of rest.

First, a hose connected to a water supply fills the wringer washer's open laundry tub with steaming hot water. After adding detergent and swishing it around a bit, a mother or her daughter will drop the lightest colored and least soiled clothing into the steaming bath. Next, Mom or her helper will flip the switch that engages the gas-powered motor that operates the washer's agitation cycle.

Once that wash cycle has completed, mom and daughters remove the dripping wet clothes and pile them into a plastic basket. In each consecutive washing, dirtier and darker clothes and rags will be placed into the laundry tub and cleaned with the same water as the first load, until it is too dirty to reuse. With thrift as a hallmark of Amish life, reusing water makes good economic sense—up to a point.

DENNIS L. HUGHES

After each item has been washed in the tub and collected into a laundry basket, mothers and daughters feed the items, one by one, through the wringer's rollers at the top of the washer. After the excess water has been squeezed out, the wet garments, towels, and rags must be sorted and then secured with clothespins to an outside laundry line.

Attached by two metal pulleys, the clothesline extends from one corner outside the house to the near side of the barn or another outbuilding.

Organizing laundry in an Amish household does not occur in a haphazard manner. Symmetry of size, color, and gender guide the process. Jewel-toned dresses flap freely in the wind. Women and teens' black bib aprons attached to wooden clothespins swing nearby. With pockets turned inside out, fathers' and sons' frayed black trousers and polyester shirts take up the next open space. Thin bath towels, washcloths, and rags dry stiff on a windy day, stretched out along another section of the line. Modest cotton underwear and hard-to-clean white socks dangle separately, clipped to a circular hanger.

Laundry imposes a slow and relentless process for Amish women, completed before breakfast in some households.

One Amish mother of eight asked me how I dried our laundry, and I sheepishly responded that we use an electric dryer and sort heat- or color-sensitive garments on a laundry line in our basement. She was surprised that clothes could dry that way, and even more amazed that my husband launders our family's clothes and hangs them to dry.

Home Cooking

"I do not buy things that I could make at home," a no-nonsense Amish mother told me.

The Amish women I met routinely dissolve yeast and sugar in warm water, mixing it with flour for loaves of bread. After the ingredients rise for an hour or two, women fold and punch down the dough and ease the kneaded mixture into seven or eight loaf pans. Soft-crusted and aromatic—white, whole wheat (and on special occasions raisin)—the earthy sweet scent of homemade bread envelops Amish households on baking days.

In addition to baking bread, Amish mothers boil milk for yogurt, blend and bake ingredients for trays of granola, and roll out dough for flakey homemade pies and fat hand cut noodles. Daughters practice their novice baking skills by mixing ingredients for chewy molasses cookies and jammy fruit bars.

Repetition and close observation of mothers, aunts, and older siblings help the younger girls memorize when a dash of this should be added to a pinch of that.

Amish women also use recipes from Amish-authored cookbooks, readily available in local dry goods stores. Secured with plastic comb bindings and pliable covers, these cookbooks function as reliable workhorses in Amish kitchens. Traditional recipes for potato rolls, chicken corn soup, and Snitz pie fit neatly between inspirational verses and prayers in cookbooks simply typeset without glossy photos.

GRANT BEACHY

Snitz pie, served at every church midday meal in Lancaster County, mixes apple butter and apple sauce, spooned into a pastry shell. This recipe feeds a crowd.

Snitz Pie for Church

2 gallons apple butter
3 gallons applesauce
5 cups sugar
½ cup lemon juice
1 rounded tablespoon cinnamon

3 rounded tablespoons cloves
½ cup melted butter
1 cup Clear Jel or tapioca
1 teaspoon salt

Stir together and fill unbaked pie shells. Top with other crust. Bake at 350 approximately 1 hour or until done.

Excerpted from *Katie's Kitchen: Memories of My Favorite Recipes, Songs and Poems* (reprinted 2011). [1]

Of course, Amish women also scribble down recipes on index cards when a neighbor shares a recipe for Greek yogurt or chili soup. Those who receive a daily newspaper may try a fresh set of instructions for using common ingredients. But the Amish women I met do not seek out the latest culinary trends. Instead, they reiterate versions of traditional foods, the ones that their parents and grandparents have been eating for generations.

Like those who live outside the Amish community, Amish women have personal preferences when it comes to homemade products. One Amish mother might take the time blending graham nuts (a crunchy cereal like the commercial brand Grape-Nuts®) from scratch. Her friend might stretch out homemade granola by mixing it with store-bought cereals of shredded wheat or cornflakes. One family may purchase only organic foods in bulk while others seek out the most economical items at Costco, regardless of their origin.

> **"Do you churn** your own butter?" is a question frequently asked of Amish women by outsiders. I have yet to hear an Amish women answer "Yes."

I met one grandmother who goes to the trouble of purchasing oat groats (a whole grain) so she can mill her own flour.

"We think it is fresher and it tastes better," she said on an extra trip we made to a farm that sold burlap bags full of groats.

"I count on using a dozen eggs a day, some for breakfast, the others for baking," said a mother of eight, who had filled my car with a ½ case of eggs, 15 dozen.

Some Amish women raise chickens, while others receive inexpensive eggs from well-supplied and generous neighbors. Amish women can purchase eggs by the flat at a big box store (thirty to a flat) or at Amish grocers who sell a dozen eggs for as little as $1.69 a carton.

Amish families typically greet the morning with a hearty breakfast that could include cornmeal mush (a porridge of cornmeal cooked with water similar to polenta) or oatmeal, homemade granola or store-bought cereal, yogurt, eggs, toast, their own preserved jam, fried bacon, sausage, or pork scrapple. Like non-Amish parents, Amish fathers and mothers start their day with either a mug of steaming coffee or hot herbal tea.

"I can't imagine breakfast without mush," an Amish mother insisted.

"Why would I make a peanut butter and jelly sandwich when there is so much else to eat?" asked an Amish mother, assuming that English children frequently consume PB&J for lunch.

The noontime meal varies in Amish families just as lunch choices differ for non-Amish families. The midday meal (called "dinner" among the Amish) often begins with homemade soup. Ladled from mason jars preserved over the summer, the stick-to-your ribs soups make a quick and easy addition for lunch. I have also watched soup created on the spot with bits of last night's chicken, beef, or vegetables, a little broth, a splash of milk, and a pinch of seasoning.

Leftovers or simple sandwiches often accompany the soup, using homemade bread for the base of sweet baloney, pressed turkey, ham, or American cheese, lettuce, onions, and tomatoes. Common condiments on Amish table include jars of home-cured sauerkraut and pickles as well as home-canned applesauce served at midday and evening meals.

If a family derives its livelihood from farming, they will eat more hearty meals at noontime. Fathers and sons, having spent long mornings milking and feeding their cows or plowing adjacent fields, look forward to a substantial meal of meat or chicken, potatoes, noodles or beans, homemade bread, a big salad with grated cheese and eggs, and fresh-baked desserts.

Up before dawn, mothers and the older girls pack lunches for the students headed off to school. Amish schools lack cafeterias or vending machines. Instead of lugging books to and from school, the children carry

The top of the school's warming stove provides the perfect spot for heating up lunch items that might require it. Even first graders know which foil packages in their lunch box will need reheating after the first recess.

their insulated lunch coolers inside their backpacks. A child's midday meal eaten at school (outside when the weather permits) might include leftovers packed in foil intended to be warmed on top of their schoolhouse's propane stove, a sandwich, carrot sticks, chips, a thermos of water or meadow tea, and a scratch-baked fruit bar, cookies, or a wedge of pie.

<hr />

Back at home, supper preparation weighs heavily on mothers' minds, especially around the time the children return from school. The scholars typically fly through the kitchen door between 3:30 and 4:00 pm, after their walk home from school. The children grab a snack, clean out their lunch coolers, and change into clothing appropriate for their afternoon chores.

Mothers supervise a burst of activities in the abbreviated period before supper. The younger children might clean a pet's cage, sweep the back steps, or move provisions (like heavy jugs of cool water) from the downstairs refrigerator to the kitchen upstairs. Younger siblings take turns setting the supper table, stretching tall to reach the dishes in the cabinet, and filling the plastic drinking glasses with water. The

Amish feed large families, and burners works overtime at supper.

older daughters might start peeling potatoes, chopping lettuce, carrots, and cabbage for a salad, and lightly boiling the vegetables.

Without a microwave oven, frozen chicken, beef, or pork, collected from the basement or off-site freezer, has hopefully thawed. The main dish, perhaps meatballs, sausage links, or chicken, will be baked in the propane oven.

Amish families dine together and typically sit down to supper around 5:00 or 5:30 pm. Most family members rise before the sun and by the end of the day, they are weary and hungry. Parents make accommodations for their Rumspringa teens, who may eat in a hurry when racing off to a youth event. But typically, suppertime ties the family back together at day's end, providing a retreat and a buffer from the world outside.

"Nothing is more important than family," a twelve-year-old boy reminded me, as I joined his family in lowering my head for the silent grace.

> **Amish families** seldom eat out at sit-down restaurants. The cost is prohibitive for such large families, although evening pizza delivery might be ordered for a very special occasion.

FIVE

Feeding the Family

"FOR ABOUT FORTY dollars in seeds, I can grow just about all the vegetables we need for the rest of the year," one of my Amish passengers pointed out to me.

The Garden

The arc of Amish life revolves around the seasons, unchanged for generations. Seed shopping at the Amish hardware store or garden shop can begin as early as February. Eager gardeners reluctantly pass over seed packets that linger from last year.

When the sun finally melts the remnants of crusty snow, Amish women take note of others who may have started cultivating seeds indoors, fretting now that their own gardens have fallen behind schedule. Grooming the family garden preserves a way of life and a timeless ritual of economic necessity. Despite the blustery February weather, dreams of preparing garden plots flicker.

"By March, I am down to my last potatoes. They are a little wrinkled and soft, but they taste just fine. The really mushy ones can be saved and replanted in the early spring. I use my garden for as much as I can, for as long as I can. We can still dig up potatoes in November if there hasn't been a frost," an Amish mother of five confirmed.

Within a life of discipline and restraint, Amish women maintain an animated relationship with their gardens, carefully cultivated and doted over. The garden not only provides months of family sustenance, but it also punctuates Amish life with vibrant color. As vivid and intricate as their iconic quilts, Amish gardens burst with bold perennials and rows of blossoming vegetables. Golden evening primrose, magenta irises, and scarlet cockscomb frame a parade of ingredients for hundreds of future meals. Vines of pole beans, tomatoes, and summer squashes grow alongside bowling ball–sized heads of lettuce and cabbage, broccoli, and cauliflower.

Spring planting, summer harvesting, and fall canning override other obligations for Amish women and their children. Amish schools close early in May, releasing the children (and their teachers) for more urgent tasks at home.

Tasks of Spring and Summer

In early spring, the youngest family members pile rocks and yard debris in their wooden wagons. Small hands are perfect for weeding garden beds. As children rake out winter leaves and turn the soil, they labor in bare feet. Their soles toughen up over the summer.

"At the beginning of the summer, it hurts to walk on the big gravel stones, but by the end I don't even notice it," one teen affirmed.

Equipped with long-handled hoes, rusted shovels, and garden trowels, children follow their mother's instructions on the correct spacing of

Lush gardens supply both produce and flowers for Amish families.

seedlings: place the sprouts gently into the soil, tamp down, and then cover with rich dirt from the family's compost pile.

Alongside the stout primroses and sweet peonies, the first stalks of rhubarb, asparagus, and early spinach poke above ground. Some women raise eye-catching flowers for the visual joy they bring. Other women earn extra income by selling excess nosegays from their roadside self-serve stands. Arranged in recycled mayonnaise jars and empty half-gallon milk cartons, flower bouquets sell for five dollars if the customer leaves the makeshift vase behind (seven dollars with the container). Early spring also features the surplus from prolific berry patches, green onions bunched in rubber bands, or rumpled paper bags filled with spring potatoes for a dollar or two.

"Honk if you need more change," reads the hand-painted sign at the unattended stand just outside of Narvon, Pennsylvania.

Most roadside self-service stands rely on buyers slipping coins and dollar bills into the honor box, a small metal or wooden container with a carved out slit for payment. Some honor boxes do not lock. The ethos of the cash box assumes that customers will leave exact change or make the correct change from the bills and coins in unlocked containers.

Homemade cash boxes rely on the honesty of strangers.

From time to time, I spot an Amish child peeking from behind a traditional green window shade common in Lancaster Amish homes, watching the customers peruse the items for sale. This simple exchange of commerce transmits a core Amish value to their children—be honest, even when no one is looking.

Preserving the Spring: Peas

"Plop, plop, plop. . ."

The sound of springtime in Lancaster County begins with the patter of hard green peas dropping into wide plastic bowls.

English peas must be picked slowly, one pod at a time. Amish children learn that pinching the pea pods from the vines with their thumbnails (instead of pulling them) helps preserve the plants. Observing their older siblings, the youngest children ignore the yellowish pods, already past their prime for sweetness. The peas'

Sweet peas left on the vine too long will be bitter and starchy, hardly worth the effort of shelling and preserving them.

short harvest window requires an intense effort over a few days in spring. Within an hour of selective picking, each child holds a gallon bucket filled to the brim with pea pods.

The next step: extracting the peas from their shells. Twisting each fibrous pod and removing garden peas takes time, a task that relies on mothers and children working together. A mother might hum a church hymn while her family shells buckets of peas. Or the family chats about the chores planned for the remainder of the week.

"We are making wonderful memories for our children," exclaimed one mother after a long humid day of shelling peas.

This intimate family time offers equal parts instruction, observation, and executing the task at hand. Babies settle into the crook of their mother's or elder sisters' arms, their eyes following their older siblings as they separate peas from their pods. Toddlers eagerly join the family endeavor, where each person contributes to the best of their ability.

"They often eat as many as they shell," one mother chuckled, watching her children pop the first dozen peas directly into their mouths.

Once shelled, the children pour their individual pea collections into one bucket. At the end of the day, mom and the older girls quickly blanch the container of sweet peas in a small amount of boiling salted water. The peas turn a more brilliant shade of green in only a few seconds. Next, the peas are drained in a colander, air cooled, and sealed into quart sized plastic storage bags that mom lays flat in the downstairs freezer—frozen flat packages store more efficiently. Although a tedious and time-consuming task, families laboring together convey to children the value of shared work, the centrality of family, and the pleasure of a job well done.

The shelling of peas heralds a long line of produce preparation that will require most of the mother's and children's time for the next three months. Preserving food in the Amish community takes several forms—women can, pickle, freeze, and ferment. While the younger boys and retired fathers may be recruited for specific chores, the women bear responsibility for managing the family's provisions.

After several hours of harvesting and preserving the peas, a family could yield fifty quart-sized storage bags of legumes.

<hr />

Amish "canning" refers to the containers used for preserving food, mostly glass and plastic bags. Far removed from artisanal products tied with raffia and sold in gourmet food shops, Amish canning is an arduous and unglamorous. Weeks of laborious hours spent crouched over extensive gardens and maneuvering heavy stock pots in blistering hot kitchens lacks the romance associated with canning a smattering of provisions. Preserving the crush of fruits and vegetables that all ripen at the same time requires detailed organization and stamina.

As the spring garden begins bearing more vegetables and fruit, the children move from shelling peas to picking beets, strawberries, and the more fragile raspberries, blackberries, and blueberries, one berry at a time. Once again, under the tutelage of their mothers and older sisters, the youngest learn which berries have ripened sufficiently for fruit preserves and which should remain on the plant. Mothers ferret out tasks for every child over the age of two.

"We all help together," one mother remarked.

Once the children remove the stems and leaves (destined for the backyard compost heap), the berries will be washed, boiled, and sweetened to taste. Considered a "high-acid" food, berries can be safely canned using the boiling water method (described below), sterilizing the jars and fresh lids in one boiling pot and cooking the fruit to a thick consistency in another.

Preserving the Spring: Berries

As an oversized pot bubbles on the stove, the berries cook down with a cup or more of sugar (or sugar substitute like agave or stevia). Meanwhile, a twenty-quart stainless steel water bath canner, unearthed this time every year, sterilizes the empty pint glass jars. Mom places the metal canning lids in another pot of boiling water. The jars and lids will remain in the scalding water until the fruit preserves in the first pot have broken down into a sauce-like texture.

Saved from one year to the next, the empty glass jars (if unchipped) can be reused multiple times. The screw tops that fasten the lids to the glass rust over time but can be used again because they do not touch

the contents of the jar. Only the metal lids required for a complete seal are used only once, though some women might reuse them if they remain in good condition.

After ladling the cooked fruit into the warm jars via a funnel (leaving about a quarter inch space from the top), Mom wipes the rims clean and carefully retrieves the now-sterile lids with long tongs. She centers the lids on top of the jars and then tightens the metal ring bands around the neck of the jar (but not too tight). Using a jar lifter (rounded tongs that enable the removal of hot jars from scalding water), Mom submerges the finished Jars into the simmering water bath canner for at least thirty minutes, sealing in the preserved food and sealing out harmful bacteria.

When a mother retrieves the hot preserves, she keeps the jars upright. The fruit preserves will rest undisturbed for twelve to twenty-four hours before they are tested for a tight seal (lids will be concave) and stored on shelves in a cool dry basement. Preserving twenty to thirty pint jars of sticky fruit jam in a single day is the reward for their efforts.

Preserving the Summer: Tomatoes

During the height of canning season without the benefit of air condi-
tioning, restaurant-sized pots again bubble at capacity on Amish stoves.
Fortunate families purchase an extra cook stove—often moved outside
under a covered area—or set up in the basement. Given the number
of hundred-person gatherings hosted in Amish homes, an additional
range or prep space can be indispensable.

I joined an Amish mother and her children canning two bushels
of tomatoes, about 120 pounds, for tomato-based sauces on a stifling
hot August afternoon. The grueling endeavor—blending tomatoes into
pizza sauce or salsa, ketchup, or tomato juice—takes several concen-
trated hours over the course of a week or two. A manual food mill
secured to the supper table separates the tomato pulp from the seeds,
cores, and skins. The tomato pulp drops from the mill into the gallon
bucket that catches it. The usable tomato pulp will be ladled into huge
pots and cooked down, eventually made into a tomato-based sauce or
condiment. Cores and skin will be composted.

I rolled up my sleeves in another Amish household, using a different but equally labor-intensive process. After picking ripe tomatoes,
the mother washed, cored, and extracted the soft spots with a dull
steak knife. Each tomato was cut into quarters. The tomato quarters

Turning
tomatoes into
tomato sauce
preserves the
riches of the
summer.

JUDY STAVISKY

were transferred into a conventional two-speed blender for crushing. However, the power source for the blender (a generator) was not located in the kitchen. The mother shuttled the blender pitcher filled with tomato chunks back and forth between the kitchen area and the room with the power source, one quart at a time. While this process appears less arduous than using the manual food mill, it requires an abundance of time and patience.

"Patience is a good thing to have when you are Amish," an Amish grandmother reminded me.

Families repeat the water bath canning process used for berries with tomatoes—this time filling heated quart jars with the pureed tomato products, leaving headspace at the top, wiping the glass edges clean, adjusting the sterile lids, securing each lid with a metal ring, and then moving the jars into a vigorously boiling pot for another thirty- to forty-minute water bath.

Converting tomatoes into ketchup requires the same degree of diligence. After her tomatoes had been cored, quartered, and milled, one mother blended several ingredients like vinegar, onion salt, ginger, ground cloves, sugar, and black and red pepper into the jumbo pots boiling with a thick puree of tomatoes. I once joined a family canning their own ketchup: forty-three pint jars, hopefully enough to last until next summer.

As summer advances, preserving peaches, plums, and pears, bought in bulk or homegrown, will follow the same painstaking process, with a few additional steps. Canning stone fruits requires skinning, pitting, coring, and slicing each piece. The cooks add the fruit sections to a pot with a sugary syrup. Once again, Mom boils the jars and lids and

Sauerkraut, another staple on many Amish tables, preserves green cabbage in salt. After removing the outer leaves and coring the center (recycled for the compost pile), shredding the dense inner leaves with a hand-operated device requires moving the head up and down on a sharp, a handheld mandoline-like appliance. Packed into clean jars and salted, cabbage ferments into sauerkraut over the course of several weeks.

guides the children spooning the cooked fruit into sterile glass containers, attaching the lids and rings and settling multiple jars into bubbling kettles for their final seal, engaging the children in preserving summer fruit and traditional customs.

Safe canning necessitates a mother's sharp eye and accumulated wisdom. As she lightly presses the center of the lid on each cooled jar, the children keep a close eye again on how their mother tests for an airtight seal.

In time, the children gain more confidence with their canning assignments. The tasks assigned might be tiresome, but the fruits of their collective labor are straightforward and edible. A seasonal and yearly

Preparing cabbage to become sauerkraut.

ritual, the older girls become proficient in the nuances of proper canning. Having apprenticed by her mother's side for at least twenty years, a young married woman will take on the responsibilities of chief gardener and canner in her new home.

Preserving the Summer: Corn

An Amish family invited me for a day-long event: harvesting and freezing the corn growing in their compact garden plot. Other recruits on this day included the family's eighty-year-old grandmother, four preteen and teenaged daughters (ages twelve, fourteen, seventeen, and nineteen) and one young son (age nine).

In the cool hours before dawn, the two eldest girls traipsed up and down the corn furrows, squeezing the tips of the ears, feeling for plump—not pointed—ends. Each plant only produces two or three ears of corn, requiring both bending down and stretching up when selecting ears by hand. After choosing the fully mature ears, the girls tossed the corn into empty plastic laundry baskets Once filled to the top, the sisters dragged the baskets inside to their mother and grandmother, stationed besides two caldrons of boiling water.

My Amish friend and her mother then plunged scores of ears into scalding pots for a few minutes. Once the corn had been parboiled, the younger mother balanced on a small stepladder and retrieved the piping-hot ears with a colander that lost its handles long ago. Mother and grandmother transferred the partially cooked ears back into the laundry basket, now heavy with soaking wet husks and corn. Together, they pushed the overfilled container back outside to the next stage of the informal family production line.

The two youngest daughters positioned themselves at opposite ends of a shaky picnic table. Together, they lifted the steaming basket of corn and set it between them. One by one, the girls, along with their brother, shucked each hot ear and removed the sodden husks and silky fibers. The outer husks and sticky threads will be added to the compost pile for next year's garden.

Next, my friend lugged the baskets of stripped corn back to the kitchen, where the two older girls joined her. The eldest daughters have the job of shredding the warm kernels off the cob with corn cutters, worn smooth from years of use. This ingenious wooden device has a rounded plane that holds the ear in place and a sharp scraper blade inserted in its bottom. The girls slide one ear at a time up and down until the corn cob reaches the blade.

One must rotate the corn a few degrees with each pass, releasing the kernels from the cob. The corn becomes "creamed" after it meets the scraper. A clean bucket catches the corn kernels and its milky liquid. Once the kernels fill the bucket and cools, Mom dips a dented metal cup into the pail, collecting the soft corn destined for the freezer. She fills quart-sized ziplock bags with corn almost to the top and then meticulously squeezes out any excess air. Laid flat in the

> **Part of the canning** process includes days of cutting and cooking vegetables for soups: chicken noodle, chicken corn, chicken and rice, tomato, vegetable soup and chili in bulk.

chest freezer, the corn will be moved later to a community freezer, about four miles away. On this swampy afternoon, we packaged eighty-four packages of corn, a backbreaking but productive day.

By the end of August, when home food preservation reaches a breathless pace, Amish women will immerse themselves in the final canning project of the season: making honest-to-goodness applesauce.

Orchard to Table

As the summer winds down, Amish women purchase grocery bags overflowing with Empire, Ginger Gold, and Honey Crisp apples, whichever is cheapest. Mothers and their children wash the apples and add a little water into the same massive pots that once bubbled with the spring and summer produce.

The apples simmer until they soften. Once tender, the red and yellow apples will be scooped out of the water and placed in the bowl of a hand-cranked food mill. Like it did with tomatoes, the food mill strains out the pliable skins, seeds, and tough cores from the rest of the apple, powered by a steady hand cranking of the handle. The apple's soft pulp drops from the food mill into a clean pail. The unusable peels and seeds will be added to the compost heap. Depending on one's preference, a bit of sugar or honey might be stirred into the bucket. After sweetening, the applesauce will be ready for canning.

The same stepwise canning process used for the earlier produce will be repeated: sterilizing jars and lids in boiling water, ladling the applesauce into clean glass containers, wiping spills off the jar, applying lids and canning rings, and soaking in another hot water bath. The 80-to-120-quart jars of applesauce Amish women put up in the fall may sound like a considerable amount. But the applesauce reserve depletes rapidly when feeding an Amish family over several months.

"I usually run out of applesauce by January," one Amish mother divulged.

School hours yield again to the labor needed at home in August. The older students resume their classes for only half-days in the first two weeks of school. The younger children return to school full-time after one week of half days. Each child has played a central role in their family's food production, devoting their summers to hectic days of gardening and food preservation.

Beyond Produce

The annual spring sale on chicken, turkey, and beef from local grocers launches an even more exacting canning process for many Amish women, called pressure canning. "Putting up" poultry and beef in glass jars demands extra attention because of the products' low acidity and the ease with which microbes can be introduced.

Those who home-can poultry and beef must be meticulous with the intricacies of the imposing pressure canner pot—its gauges, weights, and vents as well as the cooling process required. The chicken or turkey will be cut into chunks (without skin, fat, or bones) and then stuffed into sterile glass jars, either raw or cooked. Similarly, beef stripped of its fat and bones gets tucked into sterile glass jars, either raw or cooked. This type of canning requires a special pressure canner pot and an understanding of how to secure the canner's lid and adjust the temperature and pressure until safely preserved. Depending on the volume of meat and poultry, this preserving process takes a few days to complete.

Women who preserve beef in jars or have freezers full of meat will also supplement their inventories as opportunities present themselves. A few Amish women described a mobile rig that periodically travels to their small community. The rig has the capacity to butcher cows who might be lame. The meat is safe to eat but not available for resale.

Food Storage at Home and Elsewhere

"It doesn't pay for us to have another freezer at home. The power it uses up is too costly, and it doesn't really provide enough freezer space," one Amish woman informed me.

Even so, her Amish neighbor who lives across the field and a mile away keeps three oversized chest freezers, one positioned on the back

JUDY SEAVISKY

porch and two others in an outbuilding several yards away. Each woman handles freezing surplus foods in the way that best fits her family.

"We eat a lot of food, and we need to keep cooking," said a whisper-thin Amish woman, always mindful of preparing for the next meal.

Determining the logistics and storage required for stockpiling the requisite provisions for a week's worth of meals demands deft planning skills.

The Amish use home refrigerators and freezers that operate on propane, not electricity. Purchasing a modified fridge or freezer for a residence without electrical power may cost an Amish customer two or three times more than the standard electric equivalent.

The basic propane refrigerator used in many Amish households provides about 30 percent less storage space than a typical electric fridge used in non-Amish households. Ironically, Amish families need more cold storage space, not less. Options for additional freezer capacity impose additional costs and layers of inconvenience.

How do Amish women refrigerate the food they need each week?

Considering the volume of food that an average Amish family consumes weekly, even an extra chest freezer or two may not provide sufficient cold storage space. When Amish families reach their freezer capacity at home, they may rent cold storage space in a commercial freezer, either within a local grocer's facility or on a freezer truck parked on a neighbor's property.

Food storage lockers can be rented at many heights.

Neither convenient nor easy, visiting the off-site freezer space becomes part of an Amish woman's routine. Tasked with retrieving food from freezer storage situated away from home, mothers undertake a familiar multistep process. Preschool children need clothing appropriate for the weather before joining the excursion to the off-site food locker. Mothers must remember the checklist of items required for the next week's meals, and another list of the location of the stored frozen foods and their locker numbers.

Once a mother dresses her children, settles them into the buggy and arranges her insulated containers, she hitches her horse to the family buggy. The open carriage ride to the communal freezer can take about fifteen or twenty minutes each way, possibly longer depending on the family's proximity to the off-site location.

After tying her horse to the metal railing outside, Amish women dodge their way around curious tourists and navigate through the store with their children in tow. Once mothers locate their bulky provisions, the women load the food into the insulated packs and

In one Amish settlement, tourists visiting the local market remain unaware that hundreds of Amish families preserve their surplus food in deep lateral lockers, out of sight of the public.

I helped one Amish mother reclaim items from her family's freezer locker: a baseball bat-sized roll of baloney, six pounds of ground beef, six one-quart freezer bags of green beans, four quart-size bags of corn, four one-pint zip pouches of fruit mush, four quart-size containers of chicken corn soup, a bulk package of chicken thighs, a long ring of pork sausage, and a container of strawberry jam—enough to begin cooking a week's worth of meals.

carry or push the frozen goods back through the store. Sometimes the weight of the frozen items requires that the family weave their way multiple times between their freezer locker and the buggy parked outside.

Renting Commercial Freezer Storage Space

"I forgot how cold that freezer can be," four of us exclaimed at the same time.

For a yearly fee, one commercial cold storage space within a food market provides families with deep freeze lockers and matching keys. The labels on the front of the lockers list the name of the father in the family: Amos King, John Fisher, Elmer Miller.

Towering nine feet high in a cavernous walk in freezer, the top row of stacked lockers can only be reached by ladder. Patrons can either freeze items at home or bring them into the grocer's quick freeze for a small fee.

Tattered jackets, orphaned scarves, and mismatched gloves hang on a rack just outside this communal freezer, hidden in the back of the store. As bedraggled as the garments have become over time, they offer needed protection against the bone-chilling freezer.

The postcard rack displaying local Amish scenes is irresistible to Amish children visiting the grocery store with freezer space in the back. While the Amish shun photographs and consider posing a prideful act, wily photographers with long-range lenses steal photographs of the Amish without their permission. The children guess which image might resemble someone they know and squeal when they recognize a neighbor.

Each timeworn gray locker—about twenty inches wide, seventeen inches high and thirty inches deep—can hold up to two hundred pounds of meat or poultry if properly packaged and neatly arranged. Some Amish families rent two or three food lockers. Depending on their availability, lockers might be assigned in different aisles, on both upper and lower rows.

For the storage customer's convenience, the store provides a couple of bare-bones wooden ladders that can be dragged between the long rows of lockers. Balancing on the wobbly stepladders while reclaiming one's frozen foods can be a daring feat.

In one hand, an Amish woman shines a pocket flashlight through a stuffed locker, clutching her ample food lists: what foods to bring home and where to find them. In the other hand, she grips the shaky ladder, missing its anti-slip safety feet. Storing and recovering food requires climbing up and down the unstable ladder multiple times, made more difficult with freezing fingers. Gaining access to the lower-level food lockers requires squatting on the floor when retrieving frozen provisions.

Off-site freezers offer large families additional food storage.

Despite her best efforts, extracting a particular item from one's icy cache becomes more challenging as months pass by. In the early summer, fruit preserves, and peas packed in the rear of one locker becomes jammed behind the frozen corn and green beans added later. Locating the stewing beef stored in the bottommost locker in another row first requires repositioning all the packages of pork scrapple, ground beef, and chicken parts.

The numbing temperatures necessitate snap decisions on rearranging provisions, especially given the distance between the top lockers on one aisle and the bottom row lockers at the other end of the freezer. The creamed corn often ends up with the dense rolls of baloney and turkey ham, the raspberry jam with the beef cubes and frozen lima beans.

Yet after multiple visits to various food lockers, I never heard anyone complain about the complexity of the task.

JUDY STAVISKY

SIX

An Amish Education

The One-Room Schoolhouse and Its Scholars

"I think going to school with only kids in your own grade would be boring," asserted one thirteen-year-old student to me.

In the half-light of a winter morning, at precisely 8:00 a.m., an energetic nineteen-year-old Amish teacher welcomes twenty-seven children into their one-room school.

Lumbering yellow buses do not transport Amish children to their open classroom. Instead, the students navigate routes by foot or foot-powered scooter, at least a mile along local roads and through pastures.

But sometimes, Amish schoolchildren must cross busy commercial thoroughfares without a crossing guard. Neon safety vests worn by the children help commuters heed the diminutive figures proceeding along the roadways that bisect their community.

Tucked down unpaved lanes and built inconspicuously on donated farmland, Amish schools display subtle if any signage on their spare exteriors. But everyone in that Amish community knows the location of the schools.

Flanked by their siblings, Amish children's journey to school as a family provides another thread that weaves the community together—especially on arctic cold mornings. Children from one family meet up with siblings from another family and plod their way to school.

"Last week, everyone else in the family was sick and I had to go to school alone," an eleven-year-old Amish child reported in a letter to me.

Independence starts early in Amish families.

The Amish refer to school-aged children as "scholars." All the scholars from one Amish family attend school together in the same one-room schoolhouse, unless a child has special needs. Many Amish communities have a classroom set aside that accommodates children with learning challenges, usually on the grounds of the regular one-room schoolhouse.

Because Amish households have several children, one schoolhouse can reach capacity with only eight or nine families. When the student body approaches thirty pupils, there will be discussions amongst the school's parents about the options for next year's students, including building a new school.

> **Even though families** emphasize speaking Pennsylvania Dutch at home, Amish classrooms, textbooks, and worksheets use English as the primary language for instruction. When immersed in a full day of English at school, those first graders at ease with the Pennsylvania Dutch spoken at home become increasingly fluent English speakers. In the classrooms I visited, the scholars learn the German alphabet in second grade and will be introduced to German language workbooks in later school years.

During a drenching rain, an Amish mother might hitch up the horse and buggy and transport her children to or from school. But not on a snowy day.

Many Amish parents share the sentiments of a soft-spoken Amish mother with four school-aged children:

"Being outside in the fresh air is the best thing for our children. You don't want them to be sickly by staying inside. I am so happy to see the children playing outside, especially in the winter."

On especially stormy days, I have noticed a handful of parents and small children hunkered down in unheated buggies lined up outside of the schoolhouse, either dropping off their scholars or picking them up. After one sudden late afternoon rainstorm, I watched an Amish father

> **Ferrying scholars** to morning instruction is not as easy as hustling children into the car and delivering them minutes later to the school. Just like a trip to the off-site freezer or grocery store, when an Amish mother offers her scholars a lift to school on a rainy day, she must harness the horse and hitch it to the buggy, feed, dress, and bundle up the preschool children for the open carriage ride. The Amish do not enroll their youngest in day care or nursery school. Prior to first grade, children remain under their mother's full-time care at home.

with soaking wet pants and barn boots slosh across a muddy field, his oversized umbrella held aloft. Dripping wet, he collected his three children from the schoolhouse porch. They slogged back home, drenched, traversing through the sodden pasture, together. Sharing discomforts makes them a bit more bearable.

Amish school buildings evoke a bygone image of a lone schoolhouse in a child's simple line drawing: a rectangle topped by a triangle roof, crowned by a small cupola protecting the schoolhouse bell.

Despite the featureless visage of the school buildings, cheerful posters, colorful maps, and inspirational messages decorate the inside of Lancaster County schoolhouses.

"Amazing Things Happen When You Try," exclaims balloon letters on a poster in one school.

"Life is Not about Being Perfect but Giving Today Your Absolute Best," affirms the stenciled lettering on another school wall decorated with removable decals.

A ten-foot banner with dromedary camels, Mount Rushmore, and the Great Wall of China reads "Let Learning Take You Around the World."

Typical Amish schoolhouse in Lancaster County.

JUDY STAVISKY

130

Unlike public schools, Amish schools make references to God in the classroom as well as in the hymns sung in school.

Despite references to God, the teachers do not provide instruction on religion beyond opening every school day with a recitation of the Lord's Prayer

Messages written neatly on index cards hung in one Amish school:

"I was made in his likeness, created in his image for I was born to serve the Lord."

"With God, all things are possible."

"God made me special."

and a reading from the Bible (King James Version). The teachers may select any scripture reading but must do so without comment.

Parents and the church community assume primary responsibility for religious education. Instead of teaching religion, the heart of each school day reinforces the essence of being Amish at home and at school: having self-discipline, demonstrating fellowship, and displaying humility.

Pivotal Role of Parents in School Life

The overriding significance of parents shapes every aspect of school life. Parents' role transcends far beyond volunteering in the classroom.

"Some of the World's Greatest Parents" headlined one school's large bulletin board. Beneath it, each parent's first and last name in upper case letters, had been glued to eight by ten–inch pieces of construction paper. The names of the mother and father of the teacher and the teacher's helper were featured as well.

Within the Amish community, the children refer to adults by their first and last names, not Mr. or Mrs.

Parents drop by their scholars' school several times a year, unannounced and often accompanied by their preschool children. Visitors enter the schoolhouse unobtrusively and settle into folding chairs available for such visits, in the back of the room.

"Would you sign our Guest Book?" one of the scholars asked me during a visit, only after he had raised his hand requesting permission to do so.

Each visitor signs their name, the date of visit, and adds an appreciative comment in the back of the Guest Book binder. Filled with plastic sleeve pages designed by each scholar, the Guest Book offers visitors a brief glimpse into the lives of each student. The children personalize their designated page, responding to the teacher's helpful prompts.

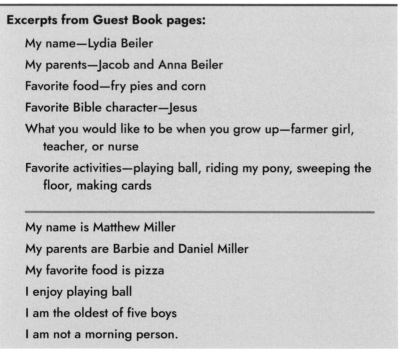

Excerpts from Guest Book pages:

My name—Lydia Beiler

My parents—Jacob and Anna Beiler

Favorite food—fry pies and corn

Favorite Bible character—Jesus

What you would like to be when you grow up—farmer girl, teacher, or nurse

Favorite activities—playing ball, riding my pony, sweeping the floor, making cards

---

My name is Matthew Miller

My parents are Barbie and Daniel Miller

My favorite food is pizza

I enjoy playing ball

I am the oldest of five boys

I am not a morning person.

When guests arrive, the scholars finish up their current assignment and then line up in the front of the schoolhouse in preparation for the welcome guest "singing."

The teacher distributes songbooks that she has cobbled together. In the schools I visited, bare-bones copy machines hooked up to twelve-volt batteries reproduce the songbooks as well as the scholar's daily worksheets. (I learned that occasionally the copy machine will be housed in the teacher's home.)

Either the teacher or a designated child selects the page that corresponds to the three or four hymns chosen for the ten-minute performance. The scholars sing together without music or instruments. Delivered sweetly and mostly in unison, the songs have Christian-themed messages. Having sung the same songs of praise repeatedly over the years, the older children recite the verses from memory. The eighth-grade girls sing more robustly than their male counterparts, a few of whom look down at their feet.

Excerpt from one school's welcome song:

Meet Me There, by Frances J. Crosby [1]

> On the happy, golden shore,
> Where the faithful part no more,
> When the storms of life are o'er,
> Meet me there;
> Where the night dissolves away
> Into pure and perfect day,
> I am going home to stay—
> Meet me there.
>
> *Refrain:*
> Meet me there, meet me there,
> Where the tree of life is blooming,

Meet me there;
When the storms of life are o'er,
On the happy golden shore,
Where the faithful part no more,
Meet me there.

If parents arrive at various times during the same day, then sets of songs will be sung for each visiting parent. Drop-in relatives are not considered a disruption. Rather, the teacher and the class view hosting parents and neighbors as a privilege. A few students flash a quick grin when they recognize someone they know.

The one-room schoolhouse fortifies the powerful connection between school, family, and community. School reinforces the lessons learned at home and in church—obedience and discipline—as families incorporate the teachings of the church into daily life, each layer safeguarding the Amish from the outside world.

"Melvin was so happy to start school today, he ran part of the way there," said an Amish mother, reporting on her youngest child's first day of school.

Amish children begin school at six years old, in first grade. If a child will turn six within the first sixty days of the school year, they may be accepted into the first grade as well. Preschoolers with their mother typically drop by during the school day for a few preliminary visits before becoming official first graders the following year.

A teacher will assign homework only when a scholar struggles with mastering a basic concept. The children's chores take priority after they return home.

Scholars will remain in the same one-room schoolhouse until the end of eighth grade, their last year of formal education. Unless a family moves their home beyond the school district boundaries, an Amish scholar will attend school in the same classroom for all eight years.

The Amish Schoolteacher

"Good morning, Gideon, good morning, Rebecca, good morning, Anna. . ."

Every morning, this Amish schoolteacher greets each member of her class.

Typically female, unmarried, and in her late teens or early twenties, the Amish teacher bears the significant responsibility of instructing up to thirty children in eight different grades over a six-hour school day.

She will be assisted by a teacher's helper, who could be one of her sisters. If a sister is not available or interested, another adolescent girl around sixteen or seventeen years old will be recruited and assist a few days a week. Neither the teacher nor the teacher's helper has earned a high school degree.

Not every Amish teacher lives within the same school district as their students, but it is handy when they do. If a teacher lives outside the school district boundaries, the school's parents hire an English driver who shuttles the teacher back and forth each school day. Collaboration between Amish communities helps spread out the expenses for drivers who transport a few teachers at a time to and from the Amish schools scattered throughout the settlement.

Experienced Amish teachers offer workshops for new teachers over the summer and periodically throughout the school year. These instructor trainings offer time for honing skills in classroom management and teaching difficult concepts.

Young teachers develop reciprocal and respectful relationships with the scholars' parents, who are often neighbors or relatives. Like non-Amish teachers with advanced education degrees and formal training, Amish instructors share the progress of and concerns about each child in regular reporting periods. In return, the parents value the young teacher's insights about their child.

> **Any Amish parent** may attend the teacher training workshops.

"I am not a big one for meetings, but school meetings are a duty because we are involved in our schools. The parents run the school, they hire and fire the teacher, and elect the school board. There is very much parental involvement in our schools," emphasized one Amish father.

Amish schools do not employ school nurses. An Amish teacher's duties may include helping a first grader with diabetes read their blood sugar level after a finger prick or changing the bandages on a fresh wound of another child.

While the occasional workshops from more experienced Amish teachers provide tips on managing the classroom and teaching phonics, young teachers rely heavily on their own experience as Amish scholars and on the teacher's edition of the students' workbooks.

"The Amish approach to instruction and learning is the most conservative part of our culture," one parent maintained.

Most of the time, Amish students learn the old-fashioned way: by repetition and by rote. During reading lessons, some scholars murmur silently at their desks while others memorize spelling words on flash cards with the teacher in the front of the room. In one school, I spotted vocabulary and math flash cards cleverly stuffed into the plastic pockets of a hanging shoe caddy.

Fourth graders memorize multiplication tables in the afternoon, while other grades cipher through workbooks or memorize metric tables. Children that catch on more slowly might work with the teacher's helper in a corner or outside, even in the winter. The teacher's helper often makes a game out of a remedial drill, and children will shout out the answer and jump in the air.

Scholars routinely raise their hands seeking permission to use the outhouse, take a drink of water from their thermos, or return a book to the shelf. Being a student in an Amish school requires forbearance. The children learn quickly that it may be a while before the teacher, who is engaged with other students, recognizes a raised hand.

Using gender-specific outhouses instead of an indoor bathroom is common in an Amish school. Outhouses can be built less expensively than installing indoor plumbing. Located within the school yard but outside the classroom, boys and girls have clearly marked outhouse entrances. More pristine and comfortable than Port-a-Potties, each outhouse area provides an enclosed bench-like toilet seat, toilet paper, and hand sanitizer.

One Amish teacher's posted Classroom Rules for the school year:

1. Do unto others as you would have them do unto you

2. ONLY one person in the bathroom at one time

3. No whispering

4. Only one person out of their seat at a time

The scholars race to their assigned seats immediately after coming in from one of three daily recesses. Classroom routines do not generate groans or much feedback at all. Still, out of the teacher's line of vision, a few boys might poke one another or place their foot so another male classmate might stumble. From time to time, I have observed a couple of older girls whispering or trading school supplies.

Nevertheless, Amish classrooms operate on a bedrock principle, as one Amish mother described:

"Respect for your teacher reflects on your family and community. Working hard in school is expected of all our children."

Comportment in the classroom seldom interferes with teaching.

Special School Days

Just like public and parochial school instructors, Amish teachers prepare lessons, hand out tests and quizzes, and organize celebratory events.

One teacher surprised the scholars with cookies and milk on the hundredth day of class.

Another teacher rewarded her students' conscientious work with a treat of doughnuts and hot chocolate.

At Christmas, schools might host a "Pollyanna," when each scholar randomly selects a classmate's name and then purchases or makes a small gift for that person. Fathers and mothers attend the Christmas luncheon with their children, an event often held at the teacher's home. Every scholar's family contributes a dish. Menus include platters of cheeseballs and crackers, gallons of fruit salad, veggies and dip, snack mixes, cookies, and juices.

"Every parent is expected to attend. They would need a *very* good reason not to be at the Christmas luncheon," a younger mother stated.

Students at one school celebrated Pet Day during the final week of class. On the designated half day, scholars packed their pets into crates and hauled them to school.

In anticipation of a scheduled pet parade around the school yard, the scholars released their animals—which included a pig named Bacon, one rooster and one hen, two barn cats, and a scruffy dog. The pig could not be corralled into the procession and instead found much joy rooting around in the schoolyard dirt. The hen laid an egg that splattered on the ground, the runny yoke more appealing to the dog than any parade route. The cat had an upset stomach, probably from the bumpy ride to school, and spit up its breakfast.

While the scholars were tickled by their animals' commotion, I learned that Pet Day will not be repeated next year.

The annual year-end school picnic is a highlight and a revered custom in Amish communities. Mothers bring an array of Amish comestibles, fathers take leave from their jobs for the entire day, and families of spectators either participate in or cheer on the yearly father/scholar baseball game.

The school committee or school board, composed of a group of scholars' fathers, selects the teacher, provides periodic feedback, and arranges payment and transportation for the teacher's services. Though one playful Amish mother clarified that "The men are officially on the committee, but their wives offer their opinions, too."

The committee collects an annual "school tax" from the parents of each scholar. Teachers are paid by check, most of which will contribute to her family's general household expenses. Typically, the teacher's parents preserve a percentage of their daughter's paycheck, often depositing it into a saving account for her future.

The Amish pay all state, federal, and local taxes, with one exception. Because the Amish decline to collect Social Security as elders, Congress released them from paying into Social Security and Medicare in 1965. However, the Amish pay both local public school taxes required by their township or state and the extra school subsidy that covers the costs of operating a separate Amish school.

A Typical Day in Amish School

"Yesterday, we had Math, German, Cursive, English, and History. We are learning a lot of interesting stuff in History, such as fishing lands, the clothing people wore, and all the different kinds of languages."
—From a letter sent to me by an Amish scholar

When the teacher tugs on the long cord attached to the bell on the roof announcing the beginning of the school day, the scholars scurry inside.

Red, blue, or green scooters, tipped to one side, line the inside of the cyclone fence that defines the school's perimeter.

"We can't afford a scooter for all seven children, so they learn to share," one Amish mother said. Amish scooters can cost between two hundred and fifty dollars and four hundred dollars, depending on the type of handlebar brakes, baskets, and wheel size.

Sharing can be a difficult concept for most youngsters. But for Amish children, putting others ahead of oneself remains a virtue learned early and reiterated frequently.

The typical Amish foot scooter used in Lancaster County vaguely resembles a bike without its seat or pedals. A low frame from which the rider can propel the scooter forward with their foot connects the front wheel to the back wheel. Balancing on one foot and pushing heartily with the other, children and adults alike enjoy a scooter's efficient transport to nearby locations.

Amish scooters lined up outside along the cement wall.

After arriving at school on wet or snowy school days, the schoolchildren pad around the classroom in their stocking feet.

The teacher and her helper clip the scholars' damp gloves to a circular hanger above the stove. The children also position their soaked black shoes around the bottom of the stove in hopes of having dry footwear by the first short morning recess. Regardless of gusty weather, Amish students loathe missing any chance for recess outside.

The only heat source for the one-room schoolhouse—a barrel shaped heating stove (usually propane, occasionally coal)—maintains a snug classroom temperature throughout the winter.

On bitter cold days, children select one of the pegs secured along the school's interior wall and position their knit caps, scarves, and bulky black coats. Boys' winter clothes hang on one side of the room, with the girls' winter coats and wraps draped on the opposite side. The bright yellow neon safety vests lie under hats, scarves, coats, and sweaters. Identical red, blue, or gray lunch coolers and thermoses rest on the weathered benches that line the interior walls under the coat pegs.

"Since our children's clothing looks similar, we write their initials inside with a white marker or with a few stitches. But sometimes we end up with someone else's clothes," one Amish mother allowed.

In truth, I have spent many morning outings with Amish passengers exchanging a child's identical scarf or insulated lunch pail to the home of its rightful owner.

In one school, Amish mothers take turns bringing in lunch for the entire student population. On one such occasion, I helped a mother dispatch two different hot soups, hot dogs and BBQ sauce, sauerkraut, cut-up carrots with onion dip, popcorn and pretzels, two types of homemade cookies, vanilla caramel pudding, and meadow tea for thirty students, all delivered by horse and buggy.

During warm September days and the early months of spring, students walk to school without their shoes. Amish children prefer freedom from their footwear. As the season heats up, even the teachers provide their lessons in bare feet.

"Just part of our culture," assured one of the visiting mothers.

"We love to have our shoes off," she continued. "As soon as I can, I am barefoot, too."

A passel of children typically arrives at school before the school bell rings so they can play on the scruffy yard outside their classroom or visit with their friends.

"Our children don't have a lot of free time to play. They look for opportunities to have fun with their friends when they can," noted one Amish mother of eight.

The dirt and gravel grounds of Amish schools look remarkably similar: a pocket-sized baseball diamond and backstop, a well-used metal swing set, two outhouses or one outhouse with two entrances, and often, a storage unit for extra equipment. The girls delight in jumping rope and playing tag. The boys favor baseball. The teachers often organize games during recess and participate with the children.

Inside one Amish schoolhouse, the scholars use the old ink wells

JUDY STAVISKY

drilled into their vintage wooden desks as storage for their scissors and glue sticks. Sharpened pencils and pink erasers rest in the ten-inch grooves carved into the desktop. The children settle into folding wooden bench seats bracketed by a cast iron base. Their old-fashioned desks, also supported by heavy iron legs, have a slim compartment underneath for school supplies. Many children attach a magnetic clip to the metal side of their desk for extra papers.

Amish schools have warming stoves and wooden desks.

Seated in rows of assigned desks, the children sit quietly one behind the other according to their grade. First graders wriggle under the smallest desks in the front of the class. Lanky eighth grade boys, in the midst of their growth spurt and their last full year in school, fit themselves awkwardly under the larger desks at the back of the classroom. The teacher orchestrates simultaneous activities for each grade level. A steady buzz of children reading to themselves or working on vocabulary words provides an audible backdrop for others who might silently fill in workbooks or photocopied sheets.

I observed how younger students have the advantage of overhearing the upcoming lessons. For the thirteen- and fourteen-year-old scholars, prior lessons are continually within earshot, reinforcing concepts introduced in earlier grades. On occasion, the teacher will have the older students listen to the younger students recite a lesson. Not all older students have the patience of the teacher.

143

Dressed in shades of forest green, lavender, or gray, each girl wears a nearly identical frock home-sewn by her mother or elder sisters. Until they reach their eighth birthday, the youngest girls will wear black pinafores over their dresses. After that, a black belt apron will replace the pinafore, pinned around the back of the waist just like their mothers and older sisters.

Exchanging a little girl's pinafore with a more grown-up black belt apron marks a significant milestone for an eight-year-old girl.

Prior to eighth grade, a bonnet or scarf covers an Amish girl's head before going outside in the winter, although they do not wear coverings in their homes or inside the schoolhouse. Once an Amish girl begins eighth grade, she will fasten her first gauzelike covering atop her head when she walks to school. From the moment she fixes her hair in the morning, she will wear a covering all day. Depending on her family, some young women may take their covering off when they are at home. As customary, if it is cold outside, a rigid bonnet or knit scarf will be placed over the covering, protecting it and the owner from the wind.

The boys' solid-colored shirts reflect the same subdued hues of the girl's garments, often cut from the same bolt of fabric as their sister's dresses. Boys wear a straw hat every day except in the winter, when a dark knit cap is more appropriate. The boys remove their hats or caps when inside school or their house. In Lancaster County, the boys' black pants use black buttons, sewn along the side and top of the front panel, allowing ease of dressing. Amish wardrobes never include zippers, considered too fancy for plain people.

"Mom made us all new clothes for the beginning of school," one third grader announced to me prior to opening day, trying hard to sound factual and not prideful. (His mother stitched new clothing for her five school-aged children *before* the first day of school and between canning summer produce.)

Subjects taught in an Amish school include arithmetic, reading, phonics, penmanship, spelling, geography, history, health (not science), and German. The scholars learn hymns and sacred songs in lieu of formal music education. While playing even simple musical instruments like a triangle or a shaker is not permitted, the scholars enjoy harmonizing to selected songs in their schoolrooms.

On occasion, when the students finish their schoolwork ahead of schedule, they might draw pictures of items that are familiar to them ("free-hand art")—a fish dangling from a pole, a birdhouse amidst flowers, a pair of quacking ducks. While formal art classes are not offered in an

> Amish schools are not devoid of children's artwork, but budding artists typically sign their names on the back of their work, reiterating their humility.

Amish school, the children's drawings are all given equal prominence in the back or on the side of the classroom.

Shelves of dated encyclopedias or World Books, some from as far back as the 1970s, serve as fixtures in Amish schoolrooms. Computers, however, are not used in Amish schools—too modern and worldly even though functions like word processing, email, and accounting software may be used in some Amish businesses.

"The scholars will use the encyclopedia to write reports later in the year, and we don't need new books for that," one teacher assured me.

Several schools I visited used the *Pathway Reading* series, published by Pathway Publishers. A conservative Old Order Amish publishing house, Pathway distributes most of the books used in Lancaster County Amish classrooms. A dated collection of readers and workbooks underscoring strong moral character, the series brims with life lessons learned on a family farm. The children featured routinely haul manure, lay out fresh straw for the animals, and complete chores around the house.

Excerpts from *New Friends,* the third-grade reader, provide an insight into the how the book's main characters—an Amish father and mother—reinforce traditional Amish values to their children, Peter and Rachael:

By the time Dad was finished talking, Peter felt ashamed of himself. He was sorry he had been cross when his parents had come home from the store without bringing anything for him. He hung his head even lower when Mother reminded him that there were many hungry children in the world who often had to go without even one meal a day. 'They would be very glad if they only had what you think is just ordinary food,' she said.
(pp. 18-21)

Dad laughed. "The grass is sure to look greener on the other side of the fence. But lots of people have found that grass is grass, no matter on which side of the fence it is."
(p. 123)

Dad continued "The best thing to do is tackle our work with a will, do it well, and do it without complaining. When we learn to do that, any job will be only half as hard."
(p. 148)[2]

The teacher's edition of *New Friends*, available for anyone to purchase at the local Amish bookstore, helps the teacher guide the third-grade scholars through a list of habits. As the scholars fill in one workbook lesson, the children identify which habits are good or bad. The list of good habits includes working willingly and eating everything on your plate (or "in your lunch pail"). Bad habits include saying unkind things and asking for help when you don't need it. [3]

"If you want an Amish girl to help with chores, just give her a spray can," laughed one Amish visitor while watching the children in a frenzy of tidying their classroom at the end of the school day.

In addition to shelves of out-of-date books and encyclopedias, brooms and dust pans fill the adjoining vertical shelves. Lysol, Windex, and wood polish, along with rolls of paper towels, line a ledge within reach for end-of-the-day cleaning.

JUDY STAVISKY

The "Chore Time Chart" taped on one wall, includes a list of student's daily assignments: sweeping the wooden schoolhouse floors; shaking out the rugs; brushing off the porch; dusting desktops, stove, and doors; wiping down the windows; and cleaning bathrooms, each completed in a whirlwind of activity.

I was reminded by one visiting mother that, "even the youngest children can sweep the dusty floors and wipe the classroom sink clean."

The scholars spend the last fifteen minutes of the school day executing their assigned cleaning tasks before the clock strikes 3:00 p.m.

While the children contribute to the daily upkeep of the schoolhouse, one of the children's fathers assumes a caretaker role.

"We don't employ janitors to keep the school clean. But we do need someone to help with the repairs and maintenance. The parents vote on the person who will be responsible for two years," one Amish mother informed me.

Finding additional support for school maintenance only requires a call out to the parents for help. On a sweltering July day, I watched a handful of volunteer mothers and fathers balance on top of aluminum ladders, dusting the highest shelves and repainting the interior of an Amish schoolhouse off-white for the coming school year.

Without benefit of payment, the father selected maintains the school building year-round, cuts the grass, repairs furniture, or mends a leaky roof.

At the end of the school year, one mother with a penchant for informal bookbinding gathered other women together for an afternoon of rebinding the school texts. With strips of colored mending tape and much goodwill, the mothers reinforced the ragged spines of the book covers and inserted missing title pages into those texts that require them.

"We really don't need new books to learn the three R's, do we?" one mother said.

"I had these same books when I went to school. These are perfectly good books, and we will use them again and again," she continued, gratified that her old school volumes remained in use at her children's school thirty-three years later.

"Our Program"

"Welcome to Our Program! On December 13, 1:00 or 7:00."

The scholars carefully colored in the snowman's scarf and carrot nose on the Program invitation, announcing time and date of their upcoming school performance.

Around Christmas or early spring, Amish scholars rehearse poems and skits in preparation for an all-school performance, humbly referred to as "Our Program."

Our Program provides each student with a role in a staged production of parables, humorous scenes, tasteful jokes, and riddles.

Faded sheets strung across the front of the one-room schoolhouse divide the performing scholars from the audience of parents and friends. The teacher remains out of sight (stage right), tucked behind a short side of the bed linen, poised on a stool while balancing a binder of script lines on her lap.

Teachers pass along reconfigured and revised scripts to one another, refreshing the material every year. Novice instructors are not expected to host a program during their first year of teaching.

On this evening, both the teacher and the teacher's assistant wear the same lavender colored dresses, a sign of fidelity to one another. Attired in crisp new frocks or spotless shirts for their debut performance, the scholars squirm nervously before the curtain opens.

The students do not wear make-up or costumes, but an occasional hat, bow tie, or wooden cane enhances the skits, performed without scenery.

"Our children do not wear costumes because that is make-believe. We like to keep dressed the way we always dress," disclosed one mother to me.

While there may be a lack of costumes, in the weeks prior to opening night the scholars' mothers have been hunched over sewing machines for hours, stitching fresh versions of the same garments the children wear to school every day. There is a subtle expectation, even when four siblings attend the same one-room schoolhouse, that each child will wear new garments for opening night.

Ironically, few if any of the scholars, parents, or teachers have experienced a traditional theater performance, as either actors or audience members. In fact, the Amish eschew movies, theatrical and musical productions. Our Program offers the Amish a one-of-a-kind opportunity as spectators watching a performance by Amish children.

"The Program is a lot of work for everyone but worth the effort," said one young mother.

The performing pupils may have caught snatches of television shows while being hustled through the home entertainment section of Costco or while sitting a pediatrician's waiting room. Fathers who work in farmers markets may sneak a peek at a baseball game on another vendor's iPhone. But in general, the scholars and their families have little experience watching actors perform or interpreting a role different than the one they live every day. Until now.

Earlier in the week, the community's bench wagon will have dropped off the same backless wooden seating used at church and youth group

singings. On the day of the performance, a few fathers stack and secure the seating, bleacher style, carefully locking the benches into a
platform and then attaching one bench on top of the other in a most
ingenious stepwise manner. Older siblings usually scramble to the top
of the home-made bleachers, prime seating for Program watching. On
opening night, parents, relatives, and even visitors from other schools
pack themselves together on the familiar benches for an unobstructed
view of the children on stage.

Each Program begins with the identical opening credits: the parents.

One by one, scholars within the same family introduce themselves,
stating the first and last names of their parents. After all, mothers and
fathers assume the central role in a scholar's home and school life.
Education plays only a cameo appearance.

The bed linens open.

Three children, almost center stage, proclaim in unison, "Our parents are Jacob and Lydia Stoltzfus. We are. . ."

"Steven, grade eight," barked Steven,

"Roseanne, grade seven," shouted Roseanne,

And little Elmer, barely audible to the crowd, stammered, "Elmer,
first grade."

The Stoltzfus family children swiftly moved along, stage left. Then
the next family of scholars moves to center stage. Once again, the children announce the name of their parents and introduce each child and
their grade in descending order. The opening credits continue until
every family unit had been introduced.

Our Program unfolds into scenes that distill life lessons touched with
humor. A lengthy endeavor compressed into ninety minutes, Our

Program features as many as twenty-five poems, hymns, and skits without an intermission.

I sat in the audience during one Program where the king's character disguised himself as a pauper, testing the kindness of his subjects to those less fortunate. The one townsperson who treated the pauper with goodwill was revealed as the most big-hearted person in the land.

In another skit, "Mother's Busy Day," the children played the role of various family members and independently determined that the supper casserole needed a pinch of salt. Each relative surreptitiously added a sprinkle of salt, making the dish inedible once the guests arrived. The mother was left wondering what happened to her once-tasty dish.

Occasionally, a sequence gently pokes fun at the English. I was in the audience of one Program that included a scene where a non-Amish man could not discern the difference between a cow and a horse. Another skit featured a city dweller whose long winter scarf became entangled in an old-fashioned Amish wringer washer. Polite tittering from the audience followed.

The delivery of the children's lines sounds a bit like the scholars reciting their classroom drills, clipped and to the point. From time to time, a solitary child conquers his or her jitters and delivers a few verses of a poem with titles like: "Be What You Are" or "We Need Each Other."

Attendees do not take photographs, nor do they videotape their child's performance. Parents hold their applause until the final closing scene. The audience honors all the children together. The children do not take individual bows, nor is any one child singled out for their performance.

"You need to find the balance. You want to show the child that he has done a good job but not in a way that elevates him above the others," one mother in the audience advised me.

Our Program can be a long and demanding event for the scholars, often with two showings in one day, at midday and another performance at 7:00 p.m., with the final curtain call at 8:45p.m. Exhilarated and exhausted, the scholars easily find their parents in the audience after Our Program, who appreciate their performance in low-keyed tones.

"Nice job," murmured one mother, nodding to her daughter.

"I like the way you told the story," confirmed another parent to his son.

Unlike most Amish gatherings, this annual weeknight event offers limited time for socializing. Fatigued after long days of work and rehearsals, Amish parents and scholars face an early morning that begins well before sunrise. The slow-paced and chilly ride home in the buggy will require that parents calm down their excited scholars before tucking them into bed. The long walk to school tomorrow will require determination and a good night's sleep.

Fourteen-Year-Old School

If compulsory education in the United States mandates school attendance through age sixteen, how can the Amish terminate formal schooling at the eighth grade, when children are typically fourteen years old?

In 1972, the Amish successfully made the case before the Supreme Court (*Wisconsin v. Yoder*) that public schools exposed their children to information and ideas contrary to Amish life. The Amish asserted that public high schools offer courses in biology, chemistry, theater, and other subjects that have little usefulness or value to their community.

The U.S. Supreme Court ruled unanimously that Wisconsin's compulsory school attendance impinged on Amish rights under the First Amendment, which guarantees the free exercise of religion. The Supreme Court decision permitted Amish schools to operate independent of the public or parochial school systems.[4]

One thoughtful Amish grandmother clarified the ruling in more practical terms:

"Our children have chores and responsibilities that English children do not have. If Amish children see others who don't have those commitments, our children will begin to question our way of life. Once that happens, our community starts to unravel."

> **"Will you miss** attending school next year?" I asked a fourteen-year-old towheaded boy, three weeks after he graduated from his one-room schoolhouse.
>
> "No way," he assured me.

The Amish demonstrated to the high court that their community provides its own continuing education after eighth grade. Informal but supervised apprenticeships within the Amish community prepare teens with the skills required for rural life. Family members or neighbors offer apprenticeships to the teens, who work on a farm, in a shop, or in someone's home until they reach age fifteen.[5]

"The ruling allowed us to run our own schools within our own culture and not worry about what our children were learning," offered a middle-aged Amish father with seven children, sharing a midday meal with me and his family.

Along with the apprenticeships, Pennsylvania law requires that Amish children attend a school once a week for three hours and keep a journal of their activities until their fifteenth birthday. To comply with the law, a willing Amish adult, often married with children, hosts "Fourteen-Year-Old School" in their basement or barn. The weekly school session is alternatively referred to as "Vocational School" or "German School," because the children spend much of their time in Fourteen-Year-Old School learning German.

Weekly journal excerpts from Vocational School students:

"I washed the laundry. Then me and mom housecleaned the attic and my room. Then I brought the wash in and put it away. Then I made supper."

"I was at home today. Me and mom housecleaned the up-stairs bathroom, hallway, the boy's room and the spair room." (Instructor corrected the word *spair* to *spare* in red ink.)

"I fed the cows and washed the milkers before breakfast. After breakfast, I did my usual afternoon chores and ate dinner [lunch] and went to school. After dinner I fed the cows."

"Today I was working at Levi's as a hired boy. We were cutting and stripping tobacco most of the day. Before going home, I fed the heifers."

One vocational schoolteacher explained the reason she might request new math workbooks from the school committee. The price of gas in the math problem was listed $.25 a gallon and none of the children believed that number!

SEVEN

In the Larger World

Amish Fabric Shops

"Do you think this fabric would wear better than that one?" a married Amish woman asked her older sister, holding up two seemingly identical pieces of dark cloth.

Rubbing a swath of burgundy material between her thumb and forefinger, the elder sister was more focused on finding the right color for her ten-year-old daughter's dress.

"I think you should hold it up to the window and pull on it a bit," suggested the older sister.

The three of us—an Amish mother of seven, her sister, and I—had been examining upright bolts of fabric for nearly an hour. I have logged many trips to fabric stores that cater to Amish shoppers. Even so, I am only beginning to differentiate between the proper color and weight of material appropriate for homemade Amish garments. Amish women stitch each homemade dress, apron, cape, and nightgown for their girls; pants, shirts, and occasionally overcoats for their boys and husbands.

Because they are hidden in plain view like Amish schools and most Amish-operated shops, locating a fabric store often requires the guidance of a local resident. Minimal roadside signage crops up when least expected. The occasional "Buggy Only" parking area filled with horses and carriages might be the only indication of a fabric shop overflowing with rolls of material and sewing notions.

> **In late August,** Amish mothers must juggle sewing each child's new first day back-to-school clothing while tackling the August canning.

Amish women immediately feel at home in the fabric stores nestled in their community.

I notice a palpable quiver of excitement each time we crossed a store's threshold. Greetings and business transactions conducted in Pennsylvania Dutch provide a knot of intimacy that English stores do not. Bashful children seldom stray far from their Amish mothers, who roam the store, smiling sweetly to others in bonnets and plain dresses. Without the requirement of a photo ID or even a phone number, women dash off checks for hundreds of dollars for yards of dusky-colored fabrics, batting for quilts, and maybe a new pair of shears.

Saddled with long lists of items needed, the promise of fellowship with other mothers is an unintended benefit of such a visit. Amish shoppers can expect random reports on an out-of-state wedding or an update on an ailing parent.

To the eye of someone who is not Amish, the hunter greens, misty grays, and russet browns seem like rather bland fabric options. But watching Amish women inspect and discuss the finer points of the textiles made me reconsider my assessment. Upon closer examination, the range of appropriate colors may be restricted, but there are more shades and textures of Amish-acceptable cloth than I could have imagined. Like an assortment of Benjamin Moore paint chips with only a shade of variation between them, the fabric gradations offer choices. Proper shades of Amish cloth fall mostly into the earth tones—colors of trees, rocks, and moss—including dark blues and excluding golden yellows or crimson reds.

The women I met seemed satisfied with the variety available to them. Attuned to restricted choices, my Amish shopping companions tended toward more conservative colors if there was a shade of doubt.

"Our children learn what colors are appropriate for us and those are the ones they prefer," another woman commented as we skirted by a short row of printed cloth, and headed straight for the plain, darker fabric bolts.

Teens might desire more latitude in their fabric choices. Depending on her family and her church district's rules, a teenaged girl might select a slightly brighter hue than her mother would choose for her. One sixteen-year-old Amish teenager showed me how the inside of her dress was made of a shiny satin-like material, while the outside conformed to standard Amish dress.

> **Amish fabric stores** also sell items for English shoppers which explains the rolls of brightly colored material and velvet ribbons.

Mindful of the culture's requirement for practicality and modesty of dress, fabrics need to be both lightweight and opaque, easy to wash but durable enough to last through multiple wringer washings.

The expense of material in one store and the possibility that the fabric will cost less elsewhere presents a constant dilemma for Amish women.

"It is a little more difficult to comparison shop with a horse and buggy," one Amish mother reminded me.

Inside a fabric store, displays of needles, thread, thimbles, hem tape, and seam rippers encircle the rows of cloth. Amish women find everything they might need for a sewing project—plain snaps and straight pins for securing women's clothing, spools of dark thread and tiny buttons for boys' and men's shirts, elastic binding, hooks and eyes, and pattern cutting boards. It is a splurge to purchase buttons already in bags, pre-counted for just the precise number needed per Amish shirt.

One Amish shopper reluctantly paid for a bagful of buttons. "I should be cutting off the old buttons from other shirts, but I simply don't have the time," she said self-consciously.

Sewing and mending for families of nine or ten demand that Amish women become facile at their sewing machines (often powered by a generator). The children typically need several different sets of clothes: one for chores, one for school or work, one for social gatherings, and a set reserved for Sunday church, weddings, and funerals. The women I met estimated that their girls have seven to ten homemade dresses, each sewn by her mother or with the help of an older sister. Weekly youth group gatherings may require a couple of extra dresses for Rumspringa teens.

Always cut from the same pattern, Amish dresses look alike but vary by color. Some dresses have shorter sleeves for the summer and others have full-length sleeves for the winter. Regardless of the season, the dresses are typically made from a polyester blend, which is more durable, less wrinkly, and quicker to air dry than 100 percent cotton.

Thrift stores are the source for many neutral-colored button-down shirts worn by Amish men. Such shirts without any adornment may be worn throughout the week, but not on a church Sunday, when home-sewn white shirts are the rule.

Mothers typically replicate the boys' shirts from a pattern handed down from their mother, sister, or neighbor.

The youngest children often wear hand-me-down dresses and pants if they can be mended or patched sufficiently.

"I sew patches onto other patches, but at some point, the children need new clothes," said a mother of seven, laughing at her thriftiness.

Fabric shop owners understand that Amish women have a small window of time for their shopping excursions. Consequently, Amish fabric stores also carry home and school supplies, hymnals, marble-covered composition books, socks, underwear, black shoe polish, and hairpins. One shop has an array of women's full-length cotton slips, an undergarment that has long since disappeared from English department stores.

The well-organized basement of another fabric store stocks rows of cookware and small appliances appropriate for or adapted to nonelectric Amish homes. Cleaning products, bandannas, and hairbrushes also line the shelves. Most of the products are made in China. Ever present in Amish fabric stores are a wide selection of homeopathic medicines.

Along the walls and shelves, farm-themed toys separated by gender offer a selection of Amish appropriate non-screen amusements

JUDY STAVISKY

Playthings for boys mirror the same livestock haulers, draft horses, and barnyard animals found in Amish communities. Mini front-end loaders, New Holland tractors (a locally based international manufacturer of farm equipment), and dairy trucks look especially realistic.

Tiny pots and pans, playhouses that resemble Amish homes, and baby dolls dressed in Amish clothing have been set aside for the girls. In one fabric store's checkout line around Christmas, every Amish mother in the queue held a pint-sized dish rack with a set of plastic dishes, replicas of the drain boards and tableware found in Amish homes.

The jigsaw puzzles with images of white-tailed deer, snowy owls, and lakes lie above a shelf of board games like Pictionary, Scrabble, and Monopoly. One store featured a Christian board game called Bibleopoly, where cooperation, not cunning, is the required skill.

Christian-themed novels and songbooks for children displayed near the cash register rest alongside Amish romance novels and soft, plastic-bound cookbooks.

"We are conservative, but we do like to have fun," an Amish mother said. I nodded my head, recalling that several families celebrated milestone birthdays by hiding token gifts and endearing notes, matching the age of the celebrant. I know a seventy-five-year-old Amish grandmother who was still tracking down seventy-five gifts and cards for several weeks after her birthday.

Shopping at Amish Grocery Stores

"We need to keep these stores in our community. If we don't shop at Amish stores, they won't be around for long," mused a middle-aged Amish mother of eight.

Bordered by lush farmland and winding back roads, Amish-owned grocery stores blend into the rural landscape. A discrete sign or a handful of aging grocery carts neatly stacked outside may be the only indication of the store's unassuming presence.

Occasionally, a hand-stenciled signboard will point in the direction of "Team Parking," the designated area for horses and carriages. Parking signs guide the non-Amish shoppers who might not

> **Unbeknownst** to most outsiders, an Amish farm supply and hardware store sells refrigerated eggs, cheese, and apples, separated from the rest of the shop by heavy plastic curtains.

recognize the amount of space required for a tethered horse and buggy. While cordial to English shoppers, Amish shopkeepers may post signs discouraging non-Amish customers from photographing Amish shoppers.

Feeding large families three meals a day every day of the week (except on church Sundays) requires meticulous planning. Grocery store excursions, even locally, cannot be organized on a whim.

"We don't run out to the store for a missing ingredient," the same Amish mother assured me.

With an abundance of logistics invisible to most outsiders, food shopping for Amish women can be a titanic task, requiring painstaking organization and a block of unscheduled time. A "short trip" to the local Amish grocery store requires at least an hour or even two.

When traveling about seven to ten miles an hour in a horse-drawn carriage, the closest Amish grocery store may take at least a half hour of riding time each way, depending on the store's location. Shoppers estimate another thirty to forty-five minutes for choosing grocery items and chance meetings with seldom-seen friends. Long-time church members savor their brief conversations between the narrow aisles.

"Even a short trip often takes longer than we expect. We need to share news about our children and there are so many relations to catch up on," one mother informed me.

Waiting patiently in the one or two jammed check-out lines, behind other Amish women with overloaded shopping carts, is an exercise in forbearance and time.

The final bill could tally up to five hundred dollars or more. The Amish shoppers pay by cash or check. Again, identification is not required.

> **More Amish owned stores** permit credit card sales. These stores add a usage fee to the customer's bill or require a minimum purchase.

"Could you hold the check until Thursday?" requested one of my shopping companions.

Like the fabric store owners, the grocers know that travel to the market is not easily arranged. This time, the cashier asked for a telephone number, made a notation on the check, and, I learned later, cashed it the following week.

"These [Amish] stores don't carry a lot of items we cannot use," said an older Amish mother.

Solar sky lights and propane or natural gas lanterns softly illuminate the interior of Amish grocery stores. The propane and natural gas lighting add a bit of warmth to the interior space, a relief on wintry days.

JUDY STAVISKY

Inside an Amish grocery store, filled with natural remedies and tonics.

A dim, grainy light meets the customer at the door when it rains. For those accustomed to fluorescent-lit supermarkets, adjusting to the low lighting takes a few minutes, especially on sunless days.

Long rows of bulk plastic bags filled with baking supplies greet customers as they enter an Amish grocery store. Prices on bulk items cost substantially less than city grocers, even urban food co-ops.

"I don't need much, but you'll think I do," laughed one of my Amish passengers as we pushed two overfilled carts down the aisles.

Amish families have a taste for what Amish grocers sell. Here are some examples:

- Twenty-five and fifty-pound sacks of flour (bread, pastry, unbleached, and self-rising)

- Five- and ten-pound bags of specialty flours—gluten free and high gluten, spelt and buckwheat, organic dark rye (fine and medium), whole wheat (medium, unbleached, soft winter wheat, stone ground, and chemical free) graham, oat, and semolina

- Oats (quick and rolled), oatmeal (maple sugar and wild blueberry), and oat groats (steel cut)

- Wheat germ (raw and toasted), wheat and spelt berries, hardy red winter wheat kernels, quinoa, and grape nuts (like Grape-Nuts®)

- Donut mix (natural buttermilk and blueberry), corn meal, cracker meal, hominy, graham cracker crumbs, bran, breadcrumbs (seasoned and plain)

- Sugars (granulated white, confectioner's, raw, dark and light brown, beet and Rapadura (unrefined cane sugar))

- Obscured in the back of the store is a meager supply of commercial-brand cereals, pretzels, potato chips, cheese puffs, and tortilla chips in large economy-sized packages.

Nabisco Saltines and Ritz Crackers, both crowd-pleasers in Amish homes, are notable exceptions to generic products.

Amish mothers hoist hefty six-pound containers of corn syrup and gallons of bittersweet molasses into their carts, the key ingredients for a silky shoofly pie. A much-favored Amish dessert, shoofly pie consists of a single crust filled with molasses and brown sugar, with a crumbled topping of flour, sugar, and butter.

With a well-earned reputation for home baking, Amish women barely notice the lack of boxed cake or cookie mixes. Instead, one- and two-pound sacks of generic animal crackers, ginger snaps, and co-conut cookies suffice alongside jumbo bags of no-name fig bars and sugar wafers. Thin off-brand chocolate wafers in plastic bags, destined for homemade ice cream sandwiches, remain popular summer-time choices for the Amish.

"We don't watch television or listen to the radio, so we are probably less partial to brands then you are. If you don't want a certain brand, you can probably find what you need at an Amish store," emphasized an Amish mother as she wended her way through the store aisles.

Naomi, a wisp of a women in her eighties, remained single her entire life, residing in her parents' home. She kept a prolific collection of traditional Amish recipes like this luncheon gelatin salad:

Naomi's Luncheon Salad
    2 boxes strawberry Jell-O (or 6 ounces of granulated gelatin)
    1 cup boiling water, dissolve
    1 pint cottage cheese
    1 can crushed pineapple (16 ounces)
    1 cup evaporated milk
    1 cup crushed nuts
    1 large container of Cool Whip

    Mix together, chill. Another flavor of Jell-O can be used.

While these side dishes might be viewed as outdated by modern non-Amish cooks, Amish women whip up gelatin-based salads and desserts for special occasions. Twist ties seal one- and two-pound plastic bags of granulated gelatin used for Jell-O-type molded side dishes. Flavors span every preference: pineapple, black cherry, sugar free, grape, orange, peach lime, apricot, blueberry, cherry, raspberry, and even natural beef.

"I like Amish stores. It is easier to find the things that I need," said one Amish woman I joined on multiple shopping trips.

Items required for preparing the traditional Sunday church meal for scores of church members can be found in one or two designated sections of an Amish grocery store. Five-pound containers of peanut butter rest side-by-side with three-pound tubs of marshmallow fluff. Blocks of shelf-stable processed cheese, another staple for the Sunday midday meal when mixed with warm milk, fill a space nearby.

Discounted supplies of aluminum serving trays, napkins, coffee cups, plates, and plastic cutlery, all necessary for hosting church and youth sings, can be found piled high in the back of the store.

Behind the glass refrigerator case, ten- and fifteen-pound bricks of American, Muenster, and Longhorn line the cold shelves next to plump logs of sweet Lebanon baloney and hard salami. Cartons of eggs and eight-pound packages of lard (for pie crusts) lie nearby. Amish groceries stock ready-made tubs of frosting, fat rolls of Amish butter, and five-pound containers of yogurt and sour cream. (Note: five pounds of yogurt or sour cream is ten times larger than the eight-ounce serving size.)

Jumbo frozen juice cans can be found in almost every shopper's cart. With nine or ten family members, even a half dozen twelve-ounce frozen juice cartons only last a couple of days. Three gallon containers of ice cream, gallon packages of sherbet, and Cool Whip crowd the store's freezers along with vacuum-packed plastic bags of fresh frozen berries and peaches.

Amish-owned grocery stores carry a minuscule selection of frozen prepared foods because Amish women seldom use them. Amish families much prefer toothsome scratch-made meals.

If squeezed for time, a customer could purchase a package of frozen bake-at-home rolls or bread loaves. The scant bags of frozen crinkle-cut potatoes and mozzarella cheese sticks, the few generic frozen pizzas, vegetables and pre-made turkey burgers seem like misfits here.

Due to infrequent shopping trips, Amish grocery stores sell limited amounts of fresh meat, chicken, or seafood. Many Amish women purchase fresh beef, pork, or poultry in bulk, at the annual pre-order sales held by Amish grocers. Mothers and older daughters break down the large purchases of chickens and meat in their kitchen, rewrap them, and store the smaller packages in home freezers or in their off-site food locker. Periodically, farmers butcher healthy but lame cows and sell the meat privately at discounted prices to Amish neighbors. Trips to Costco fill in meats and poultry supplies, when necessary.

Tinned foods take up little space in Amish markets. I have rarely observed an Amish shopper purchase a can from the lonely shelf of commercially produced applesauce, pickles, jelly, or sauerkraut. Some stores carry off-brand canned vegetables, peach or pear halves, and cream of chicken and cream of mushroom soups (used mostly for casseroles).

Shrink-wrapped cartons of Ball canning jars with regular and large mouth lids almost reach the ceiling in one Amish grocery store. Resealable quart and gallon freezer bags sold in bulk provide ample supplies for preserving homemade products.

One store displays bins of various sized screw-on metal lids for shoppers interested in reusing odd-shaped jars for canning.

Herbal remedies and dietary supplements occupy much of an Amish grocer's remaining real estate. Shoppers cull through a dizzying array of herbal pills and tonics.

"We use a lot of home remedies," one Amish mother noted as I watched her reach for multiple plastic bottles of expensive homeopathic medicines and tinctures.

Lung and bronchial capsules, colon cleansers, tablets that claim to activate thyroid activity or relieve stress, dental formulas, and digestive tract detoxifiers rest on one shelf. Products advertising relief of aching joints, flagging digestion, and fuzzy memories line the space nearby. Salves for deep tissue relief, bee pollen for building immune systems, and bone enhancers rest among a slew of other health aids. Dissolvable cell recovery powder and bladder control caplets complete the row with dolomite powder, lecithin granules, and papaya leaf liquid extract.

By comparison, only a scattering of familiar over-the-counter cough medicines and anti inflammatory medications can be found, if shoppers look carefully. Assembled near the cashier and ignored by most Amish shoppers, a skimpy row of band aids, gauze, cotton balls, chap stick, throat lozenges, antacids, and nasal sprays look like afterthoughts.

There are unexpected specialty products found at Amish grocery stores: pesto garlic flour tortillas (used for lunch wraps), curry powder, basmati and jasmine rice, cappuccino mix (French vanilla, hazelnut, and creamy caramel), and avocadoes. A few stores carry Spanish paprika, jalapeño powder, taco and stir-fry seasoning blends.

On the return trip home from the store, the horse and carriage slow down as they approach the gravel driveway. The younger children carry the heaviest groceries they can manage. Numerous cartons need unloading, organizing, and stowing in the kitchen, basement, or on the winter porch. Once the children unload the buggy, their mother leads the horse into the barn. She unbuckles the multiple belts that attach the horse to the carriage, lifts the heavy harness onto its hook, guides the horse into a stall, and replenishes its water. Without giving it a thought, the mother wheels the heavy carriage into a separate section of the barn, revealing her considerable physical strength in the process.

For all her focused efforts on efficiency and time management, the day has spun away. The sliver of time remaining for supervising chores, setting the table for nine, browning the meat, boiling potatoes, and slicing vegetables for tonight's dinner dominates the mother's thoughts.

"I really don't like to be away from home for too long," a sentiment I heard repeated often by several Amish women.

Trip to Costco

"I don't know when I'll be able to return," said one Amish woman referring to Costco, "so I better buy the items I think I will need later, while I am here."

Freighted with the appeal of a big box store like Costco that offers behemoth packages, discounted prices, and restricted brand choices, Amish mothers find themselves in a constant dilemma.

"I tend to buy more than I need here," I heard more than one woman admit.

Most families have regular drivers who, for a fee, will ferry Amish women to stores like Costco. Some Amish women plan a monthly Costco trip, while others stock up before a hundred-person youth gathering.

At Costco, women shop for double boxes of cereal, twin packs of chocolate syrup and carrot juice, colossal jars of mayonnaise and olives, instant chocolate milk mix, and sixteen-ounce tubs of cream cheese along with value packs of English muffins, pistachio nuts, facial tissues, toilet paper, and paper napkins. Purchasing treats for their families at Costco, such as occasional sodas, granola bars, marshmallows, and tortilla chips, is a universal mom thing.

One of my Amish passengers left Costco with a bill for $1,233.63, paid in cash!

> **Over time**, patronizing Costco has become insinuated into Amish life for many families in Lancaster County.

> **Like so many** non-Amish shoppers, the prize of a Costco shopping trip is the $4.99 rotisserie chicken, the only prepared meal I have seen Amish women purchase at any grocery store in ten years.

On one Costco excursion, my Amish shopping companion looked perplexed as she observed a young female shopper scantily dressed in tight shorts and a pink midriff top.

"I don't understand the rule that says we [the Amish] must wear shoes into the store when the English show their legs, arms, and even their stomachs!"

Threading my way through an explanation of liability issues, I was unsuccessful in convincing my Amish companion that the rule has more to do with customer safety and little to do with revealing attire.

Amish Costco shoppers have become skilled at navigating the cavernous store.

JUDY STAVISKY

What I Have Learned from Amish Women

"WE CAN EACH learn things from each other," one Amish friend wisely told me.

After a decade of visits and countless conversations with Amish women, I remain fascinated by their uncommon grace, their unshakable loyalty to family and community, and their enthusiasm to take on hard tasks simply because they need to be done.

The list below focuses on the bits and pieces I have gleaned along the way that didn't fit easily into the preceding chapters. Ironically, this book ends where I began—wanting to know more about a group of women governed by faith, who live without pretense and are devoted to helping others.

1. Homemade Amish pizza takes many forms—including Almost Pizza (pizza dough, tater tots, ground beef, and pizza sauce topped with cheese) and Veggie Pizza (pizza dough, salad, and ranch dressing).

2. Securing a non-photo identification card requires hours of perseverance and explanations. The Department of Motor Vehicles may ask for additional papers and a return trip, creating additional expense for an Amish applicant.

3. In the heart of the Amish community, shops offer replacement parts for milking machines, metal inserts for coal stoves, and new upholstery for buggy seats.

4. Like English snowbirds, some Amish reserve bus or train tickets for winter vacations in warmer parts of the country, such as Pinecraft, Florida, a Sarasota community that caters to the Amish.

5. Amish women find background music in retail stores distracting and annoying.

6. Purchases of cupholders crafted especially for buggies turn out to be a perfect gift for teenage Amish boys.

7. Bridal registries are becoming more common in stores that serve the Amish community.

8. Bridal dresses mirror the same pattern as an everyday dress and stitched in the same subdued colored fabrics—but *never* in white.

9. Amish weddings often host between three hundred and four hundred guests. Brides are not expected to send follow-up thank you notes for wedding gifts.

10. Rings are not exchanged at Amish weddings.

11. In keeping with tradition and to ensure that families do not compete with one another, the Amish serve the same midday meal at *every* wedding: chicken and stuffing, mashed potatoes and gravy, creamed celery, and a vinegar and sugar coleslaw. Mothers, church ladies, and relatives help prepare two huge wedding meals—one midday (dinner) and one for the evening (supper). However, the evening meal can be as varied as lasagna or soup and hot sandwiches.

12. The Amish have the option of voting in local and national elections, but most chose not to do so.

13. "Amish Mud Sales" are benefit events raising funds for local fire departments. Those fire companies depend on Amish men as volunteers. Typically held during the muddy spring (thus the name), mud sales auction donated quilts, Amish-made furniture and crafts, farm supplies and equipment (even buggies). All visitors welcome!

14. The knit triangle scarves worn by Amish women in the winter are called "bandannas." Amish refer to the men's Sunday black hats as "telescope hats."

15. Over years of sharing lunch tables with their non-Amish co-workers, Amish men have developed a taste for hot sauce, now more common in Amish homes. Home canning recipes often include batches of salsa.

16. When treating common ailments, the Amish often seek advice from family and alternative health providers. However, some Amish will visit a medical doctor when necessary.

17. When a family member requires hospitalization at a distant medical facility, unsolicited contributions from the Amish community

pour in and help defray the expenses. Most Amish do not have health insurance coverage.

18. Amish girls love sleepovers!

19. Displayed in a makeshift booth outside their home, Amish children paint outgrown metal horseshoes (from the family's horse), anticipating sales to back-road tourists.

20. One of the questions the Amish are asked frequently and find most puzzling: "Do you like being Amish?"

ACKNOWLEDGMENTS

— ॐ —

I AM DEEPLY indebted to the Amish women, men, and teens who graciously shared their thoughts, opinions, and time with me. I have tried to represent their lives with honesty and respect for the confidences they shared. I am also most appreciative for the Amish colleagues who read parts of my manuscript and offered suggestions.

The following people have provided invaluable support in preparation of this book. First, my husband Alan Schiff, who offered his unconditional encouragement and guidance throughout this process. My visits with Amish women took place over ten years. Alan's fascination and commitment to this process was matched only by my own.

For a decade, Donald Kraybill has been as generous with his advice and counsel as he is knowledgeable about the Amish. This book would have remained a dream without his enduring support and genuine interest.

Early on, Mary Geitz, a seasoned writer herself, reorganized my random collection of experiences with an expert hand. Several friends encouraged me across the finish line throughout this lengthy process: Sandy Sherman, Debbie Erenrich, Michael Gillian, Lynn and Hank Paper, Alison Shaw, Derk Jaeger, Harriet Baskin, Ruth Isenberg, Jeanette Lucey, Constance Touey, Janet Mason, Jan Weschler, Rhona Weiss, and Fern Zeigler.

Thank you to Steve Nolt, Cynthia Nolt, and the Young Center for Anabaptist and Pietist Studies for their wealth of resources and nimble response to inquiries. Rachel M. Grove Rohrbaugh, Archivist at Elizabethtown College culled through scores of Amish community images to support this book. My gratitude to Dennis Hughes, whose gift for capturing the subtilties of Amish life demonstrates his sensitivity and affinity for the subject.

I am grateful for the support of our growing family—Evan, Bonnie, and Lyla—who always knew I was working on something important. And to my dad, Samuel Stavisky, a former *Washington Post* reporter and author at age eighty-five, who stressed the power of sharing stories.

DENNIS L. HUGHES

NOTES

Call from Leah

1 Donald B. Kraybill, Karen M. Johnson-Wiener, and Steven M. Nolt, *The Amish* (Baltimore, MD: Johns Hopkins University Press, 2013), 333.

Chapter 1

1 Donald B. Kraybill, Karen M. Johnson-Wiener, and Steven M. Nolt, *The Amish* (Baltimore, MD: Johns Hopkins University Press, 2013), 30.

2 Kraybill et al., *The Amish*, Chapter 2.

3 "Twelve Largest Amish Settlements, 2021," Young Center for Anabaptist and Pietist Studies, Elizabethtown College, accessed February 20, 2022, http://groups .etown.edu/amishstudies/statistics/twelve-largest-settlements-2021/.

4 Steven M. Nolt, *The Amish* (Baltimore, MD: Johns Hopkins University Press, 2016), 17, 83–84.

5 John A. Hostetler, *Amish Society* (Baltimore, MD: Johns Hopkins University Press, 1993), 82–83.

Chapter 2

1 Donald B. Kraybill, Karen M. Johnson-Wiener, and Steven M. Nolt, *The Amish* (Baltimore, MD: Johns Hopkins University Press, 2013), 175.

Chapter 3

1 "Frequently Asked Questions," Young Center for Anabaptist and Pietist Studies, Elizabethtown College, accessed February 20, 2022, https://groups.etown.edu/ amishstudies/frequently-asked-questions/.

2 "Census Bureau Releases New Estimates on America's Families and Living Arrangements," November 29, 2021, United States Census Bureau, https://www. census.gov/newsroom/press-releases/2021/families-and-living-arrangements.html.

Chapter 4

1   Katie Fisher, *Katie's Kitchen: Memories of My Favorite Recipes, Songs and Poems* (Bird-in-Hand, PA: 1995), 53.

Chapter 6

1   Frances J. Crosby, "Meet Me There" (1885).

2   *New Friends* (LaGrange, IN: Pathway Publishers, 1977) 18–21, 123, 148.

3   *Workbook for New Friends, Teacher's Edition* (Aylmer, ON: Pathway Publishers, 1989), 10.

4   Steven M. Nolt, *A History of the Amish* (Intercourse, PA: Good Books, 2003), 306–308.

5   Donald B. Kraybill, Karen M. Johnson-Wiener, and Steven M. Nolt, *The Amish* (Baltimore, MD: Johns Hopkins University Press, 2013), 267–269.

ADDITIONAL RESOURCES

— ࢨ —

Hostetler, John A. *Amish Society*. Baltimore, MD: Johns Hopkins University Press, 1993.

Kraybill, Donald B. *Simply Amish*. Harrisonburg, VA: Herald Press, 2018.

Kraybill, Donald B., Karen M. Johnson-Weiner, and Steven M. Nolt. *The Amish*. Baltimore, MD: Johns Hopkins University Press, 2013.

Kraybill, Donald B., Steven M. Nolt, and David L. Weaver-Zercher. *The Amish Way: Patient Faith in a Perilous World*. San Francisco, CA: Jossey-Bass, 2010.

Kraybill, Donald B. *The Amish of Lancaster County*. Mechanicsburg, PA: Stackpole Books, 2008.

Kraybill, Donald B. *The Riddle of Amish Culture*. Baltimore, MD: Johns Hopkins University Press, 1989.

Nolt, Steven M. *The Amish*. Baltimore, MD: Johns Hopkins University Press, 2016.

Stevick, Richard. *Growing Up Amish. The Rumspringa Years*. Baltimore, MD: Johns Hopkins University Press, 2014.

Tice, George. *Fields of Peace*. Jaffrey, NH: David R. Godine, 1998.

Young Center for Anabaptist and Pietist Studies, Elizabethtown College is a nationally recognized academic site for Amish related information and data, updated annually. https://groups.etown.edu/amishstudies/.

THE AUTHOR

— 🦢 —

JUDY STAVISKY, MPH, MEd, has spent considerable time over the past decade attending Amish schools, sharing meals with Amish families, and joining events hosted in the Amish community. Judy has a lengthy career in philanthropy and helping nonprofit organizations become more successful. She is co author of *Do It Better! How the Kids of St. Francis de Sales Exceeded Everyone's Expectations*, chronicling the journeys of Philadelphia's student refugees. Recently Judy has been supporting the city's refugee resettlement efforts, connecting food insecure Philadelphians with meals. She is an adjunct faculty member at Drexel University.